NOTHING
TO
FEAR

First published in 2010 by Bellwether Press, P.O. Box 1110, Florissant, MO 63031. Distributed by House of Penguin, USA www.houseofpenguin.com

Library of Congress Cataloging-in-Publication Data

Elmashhady, Hady

Nothing to Fear: Seven Simple Steps to Transcend Anxiety / Hady Elmashhady.

  p. cm.

  ISBN: 1-45151-116-7

  EAN-13: 978-145151116-1

  1. Anxiety disorder. 2. Overcoming fear. 3. Self-help — miscellanea. 4. Arab-American writers.

Edited and Designed by Joachim Alexander
Printed in the United States of America
10 9 8 7 6 5 4 3 2 1

NOTHING TO FEAR

Seven Simple Steps to
Transcend Anxiety

HADY ELMASHHADY

To my parents,
Hany and Hanaa,
and to all who suffer with an
Anxiety Disorder.

Contents

AN ANXIOUS LIFE

When you live with anxiety, life itself is a chore; no longer something to be enjoyed. You simply go through the motions, and every day is the same as you exist in a near constant state of worry. People with serious anxiety problems can't truly live their lives fully. Those who have not experienced anxiety disorders could never hope to understand them. They just don't know what anxiety sufferers experience, because anxiety isn't something that can be realized with the normal senses — such as touch, sight, or smell — in the same way that a physical ailment such as a wound or tumor can.

I know what people with anxiety experience on a day-to-day basis. I know the depths that people can reach when they have an anxiety disorder. I know how alone someone can feel when they are suffering in this way. I know, because I was once an anxiety sufferer, and to put it short, it was a real bitch. Judging by the fact that you are reading this, it is safe to assume that you have some sort of anxiety problem and wish to be rid of anxiety, and its remnants, once and for all.

You've probably looked for answers in all sorts of places. You may have visited therapists or even psychiatrists who prescribed drugs to help "ease" your "symptoms." Or maybe you're the type of person who simply just sucks it up and deals with these awful feelings and sensations inside of you. Whatever the case, all that matters is that you want to be well. If you read this book with the intention of using the information in it, and act upon the steps as they are presented, you will be well. That is a promise from me personally. Believe me when I say that I know how you feel, and I want you to be well.

Let me begin by saying that I do not make a living as a psychiatrist, psychologist, or even as a lay-therapist. I am not going to bog you down with fancy terminology or things only these professional practitioners understand. Such methods will not help or benefit you in any way, as I'm sure you have likely experienced at some point. However, I am going to give you detailed and simple steps to follow with explanations and advice that will help you to be well again. I can say this because I am a person who was in the same boat you are currently in, and have used these same methods myself.

All of the tools you will need are in this book as well as inside of you, as you will quickly find out. I used to have anxiety, and I figured out how to beat it on my own. You will learn the techniques and methods that I have utilized, and will hopefully use them to help you rebuild yourself. You can trust this information knowing that what I have to offer is cold, hard *experience*.

I have sunken to the darkest depths of my own anxiety disorder and have learned a lot about myself and how my mind operates in the process, and you will too. The point, plain and simple, is that I know that the feelings of anxiety are utterly appalling and I do know exactly how you feel. You may feel things ranging from shyness all the way to abject fear. You may have even experienced panic attacks. Anxiety shows itself through symptoms that vary from person to person. However, the symptoms don't really matter. Anxiety is anxiety.

As a small child, I was nearly always happy. I had many friends and all seemed well. I earned mostly A's in school and had good friendships and family relationships. However, I felt as though I had this curse shadowing me. I never really understood it or thought about it, but I knew it was there. I just felt that something wasn't right, because I couldn't control certain feelings sometimes. Feelings like fear, guilt, worry, sadness, and anxiety seemed totally beyond my control, and at times would almost consume me.

Sometimes as a young child, I would become frightened of small things. Little things like being scolded by a parent or teacher in elementary school would really frighten me and make me feel guilty inside, and I would hold on to the feeling of guilt for quite some time after. I would beat myself up over every mistake I made and would feel truly guilty for long periods of time.

I knew that I wasn't supposed to feel this way, because nobody else seemed to. My anxious behavior as a child never really lasted any particular length of time, and it would subside eventually. In fact, the anxious feelings didn't happen very often, but when they did, boy were they bad. As I would find out before too long, I had an underlying anxiety disorder. However, I had not realized it or how bad it was until shortly after my seventeenth birthday when it finally dawned on me that I suffered from an anxiety related condition.

For years I exhibited anxious behavior, but it hadn't gotten as bad as it did until this point, when I suffered my first panic attack. In my mind I was having a heart attack. It was fairly sudden. I began to feel palpitations one night, and a small pain in my chest caused me to worry excessively. My mind fired away with the idea of an imminent heart attack.

My head was flooded with images of my heart beating vigorously in my chest while blood was shooting out of the muscle. I even felt a pain in my left arm, and it felt as though hot lead was coursing through it. I literally thought that my heart was going to explode.

I imagined myself in the emergency room that night, dead. All seemed hopeless, but for whatever reason I didn't want to call an ambulance, and I decided I was just going to try and live through it. This was mainly due to my secretive nature at the time. I didn't want anybody to know, so I just hid it away.

I'm a pretty fit guy, and at the time of this panic attack I was just as physically fit. However, I completely overlooked the fact that it was almost impossible for me to have a heart attack since I live an active lifestyle. However, I believed it, and that's all it really takes. Once this subsided, I felt a tightness in my chest for a week or two afterward. I began to believe that my heart was injured in some way, or even failing.

A few weeks later I began to experience the most horrific chain of events that ever took place within the depths of my mind. You know the feeling you sometimes get that you are dreaming, even though you aren't; that feeling where nothing seems real? That's what I was experiencing. But it was different in my case, because it persisted. I slowly descended into an intense sense of unreality. In other words, everything that I saw in front of me felt like it wasn't real, like I was dreaming, or watching a movie.

Nothing felt real or substantial in any way. Nothing had purpose, merit, or even a reason for existing. I experienced this numerous times before, but it never lasted. Sometimes I would feel it when I would wake up early in the morning or just at random times. There was no pattern.

This time it was different, however, and became locked in place, lasting a long time (I'll explain why this happened later in the book).

This was absolutely horrific for me, because I had no idea what was going on. I mean really, I was just fine the day before, and now this was happening! I thought I was going nuts. I would look at my hand, and it wouldn't feel like it was mine. My whole body didn't feel like it belonged to me, and at times I felt as though I was floating outside of it. I just didn't feel right in my own skin.

At other times, I would even look in the mirror and strain to remember who I was. This was what really scared the living hell out of me. I felt like I was looking at a stranger and I truly couldn't recognize myself. And sometimes I would even feel absolutely nothing. Zero. I literally lost my ability to feel much of anything at all emotionally. I'd have a total loss of my own sense of personality, and nothing seemed to matter more than what I was experiencing in those moments. It was pretty tough.

As I mentioned before, I tended to be a secretive person, never letting others know anything about my feelings or thoughts. So being the way I was, I concealed it — another no-no that I will discuss later — and did my best to act the way I normally do so I could keep others from knowing.

I went about my way as usual, from my duties at home to those at school. I immediately began looking for answers, searching tirelessly online and in books about what was going on with me. After spending countless hours researching anxiety disorders, it seemed appropriate to research the brain itself.

I learned about the make-up of the brain, how it works, and why people do the things they do. I learned about the primary part of the brain that is involved with what we know as anxiety, which we'll explore in-depth a bit later.

Then, I began surfing the web diligently to find an explanation for all of this. As I hunted for a name for what I was feeling, I finally found it. My computer screen read:

> *Depersonalization Disorder consists of persistent or recurrent feelings of being detached from one's body or mental processes, usually with a feeling of being an outside observer of one's life.*

That hit the nail on the head, and I read on. The symptoms were exactly what I experienced; namely, the dreamy, unreal feelings, like I was watching a movie or something. This deepened the condition even more, because I now began to fear that I had some kind of mental illness. All efforts to find a way out of this seemed hopeless and futile. However, I felt it must be beatable because it had periods of remission, when everything would feel "real" again for a moment or two.

Although these periods would last for very short lengths of time, they proved to me that there was indeed a solution somewhere. This Depersonalization was to last for eight straight months.

This was a truly frightening time in my life because I am someone who likes to have a tight grip on reality. I tend to be a very logical person, always analyzing and trying to explain things. Feeling like I was crazy all of a sudden was something I could not swallow. Thoughts crossed my mind that I was "losing it" or that I was even in the first stages of becoming psychotic and, to say the least, I was absolutely terrified. Nothing made sense to me anymore.

I dwelled on this "unreal" feeling for a very, very long time, and it caused me extreme mental anguish. I remember just standing there in the shower one morning, holding my head and just feeling completely terrible. I just could not believe what was happening to me. I truly began to accept that I was losing my mind.

As I searched and searched for a cure of some kind, I figured out positive ways to help me cope. Vigorous exercise like lifting weights and running helped me get my mind off the anxious feelings. It seemed to have a soothing and satisfying effect on my mind. I found that fatiguing my body and mind allowed me to be distracted from Depersonalization.

Another thing that helped me with my anxiety was my true passion for martial arts. Everything about the martial arts feeds a deep, burning desire within me. It's my calling and passion. Since I first saw Bruce Lee on television when I was ten years old, I have had an unrelenting and unquenchable passion for everything about the various martial arts, the teachings, and philosophies.

Luckily, I was involved in them already. I participated in Tae Kwon Do and Muay Thai (Thai Boxing) before my anxiety began to get really bad. So I wasn't doing anything new that would make me feel any more uncomfortable than I already was, or so it seemed. Going to my Tae Kwon Do and Muay Thai practice regularly allowed me to divert my mind away from my anxiety for the time I was in class. However, as the anxiety worsened, it spilled over into my life as a fighter.

It was so weird. My desire, my passion, my very life, was now being impaired by this awful condition. The Tae Kwon Do classes didn't cause me much discomfort. The atmosphere was much more relaxed, than Muay Thai, not to mention the contact during sparring was a lot less brutal.

Sometimes I would go to Muay Thai feeling an impending sense of doom. I would feel like something terrible was going to happen as I wrapped my hands and got ready for practice as usual (key word here: *as usual*. Nothing at all had changed).

I'd look at my friends in the gym and feel like they were out to beat me up or even kill me. Obviously this wasn't the case, but in the mind of an anxious person, it *must* be true. Scenes of my body being broken in some way would flood my mind and it would truly scare me. This was when I decided enough was enough.

I wasn't going to let this control my life, and especially not my passion.

I began to force myself to go to the gym and continue to develop my Muay Thai, no matter how awful I felt. I remember sparring in the gym, and how terrified I felt at times. I literally would feel like I was fighting for my life, until the bell sounded at the end of the round and I would be relieved. Keep in mind that this is my passion. This is what I truly love to do.

Time stops when I am doing Muay Thai because I love it so much. It's just that anxiety began to affect my passion and disposition for the Martial Arts. That's where I drew the line. I remember thinking to myself, *all of this anxiety bullshit has caused me so much trouble, but seriously, no more. Sure, it sucks, but I'm not gonna let it affect what I love to do. Others might, but not me.*

Then I really started to think deeply about all of this. In my mind I thought, *Hold on a second… I've done this a million times before, why am I feeling this way now? This doesn't make any sense.*

This single thought caused a switch to click in my mind and really got the gears going in my head. This single thought would drive me when I would go to the gym or do anything else that would spark the flames of anxiety. I made the commitment to force myself into any and all discomfort no matter how bad it felt.

Sure, I put my nerves through a meat grinder, but I got through it. That was when it really clicked in my mind. Yes, it felt extremely dreadful, but it's not like it could have killed me. I still got through it every single solitary time, and afterward I would taste the most delicious satisfaction knowing that I had forced myself through it all on my own and had actually tackled my anxiety.

The anxiety and the thoughts and feelings associated with it would still occur when I would go, but for the time being I just felt secure knowing that I could beat it, because with every visit to the gym, the feelings were less intense and would seem to diminish further each time.

I knew it was only a matter of time. I normally pushed my body and mind past the envelope before I experienced these more serious anxiety problems, but now I was really beginning to see what I was made of. I began to learn what I could truly be put through and still come out fine at the other end of the dark tunnel. The main thing was that I forced myself to dive head-first into every situation that made me uncomfortable until I became at ease with (and better understood) the sensations associated with those situations.

I then began to delve further into studying the mind and how it works ranging from modern psychology all the way to ancient Zen. I studied how our minds process things through the conscious and subconscious mind. I learned how the practice of Zen can keep you calm in literally any situation if used correctly. It was amazing how much I had learned.

In fact, now I can say that I am actually grateful for having to deal with an anxiety disorder at that point in my life, because it made me stronger on so many levels, and the fact that I learned *so much* about myself was pretty damn cool, to put it plainly. I learned things that I previously could have never even begun to conceive of. All the knowledge that I gained from countless hours of independent study allowed me to reap the fruits of well-being soon after. I am actually truly grateful for this experience, because it made me so much stronger as a person. You can be grateful too, because the journey into yourself will begin, and as you heal, you will come out an incredibly stronger person, you can count on that.

Fast-forward and I completed my own healing process. The process was gradual, and it was mentally, emotionally, and even physically painful at some points. However, in the end it was absolutely worth it in every area.

After being uneasy and worried all the time due to having anxiety, experiencing depersonalization for so long, feeling that nothing around me was real, literally feeling everything from panic to absolutely *nothing* at times, and then feeling like myself again, was extremely fulfilling. I was pleased in ways that I couldn't believe. I felt like my soul ascended into heaven. I am almost at a loss for words to describe my utter relief and the peace that I felt after it was gone. The funny thing is that it was gradual and instantaneous at the same time. Let me explain.

The process by which I became well again took some time. I slowly learned how to get rid of my anxiety disorder, but my sense of reality — or the feeling of "real" — returned in an instant as I began to turn my attention away from depersonalization, and focus instead on my world around me. It felt absolutely miraculous to say the least.

Lights seemed to brighten as I started feeling better. The small details in everything like the dimples in the paint on a wall or the little fibers on a carpet really stood out and shined to me. Simple things like the pictures on the walls in my house, the way the wood floor gleamed in the sunlight, and the sight of birds chirping in the branches would astound me in unimaginable ways. It was an absolutely incredible feeling.

I felt like a veil had been over my eyes all this time, and now it fell away and turned to dust. I felt absolutely *reborn*. Everything around me seemed new and interesting; almost in the same way a newborn baby sees the world, all because it felt *real* again. Words simply cannot fully describe what I felt. My own drive to push myself and to always seek the best in me ultimately allowed me to get through this, and you can do the same. You are a lot stronger than you think you are. It is this struggle within you that will bring you mental strength and toughness that you could have never imagined, not to mention a certain satisfaction once you get there.

This story in itself serves to encourage you. I wanted to share it with you so that you could recognize where I was at during that dark point in my life. Sometimes I look back in disbelief that I was able to actually become well after experiencing such horror. You must realize that you can do the same.

You may be wondering, *Hady, how would you know how I'm feeling? You don't even know me.* I know how you are feeling for two reasons. One: You have an anxiety disorder (or know someone who does), otherwise you wouldn't be reading this book. Two: I used to have an anxiety disorder as well. Remember, anxiety is anxiety. You are reading this book because you want an end to your anxiety disorder once and for all, and with good reason. Who would want it to continue?

I want you to understand that I know how horrible it is to feel like you are going to die, or lose your mind, or something else as equally terrible. If I can become well again, you can bet that you can, too. Look where I came from, and look at where I am now. If you follow the actions recommended in this book, you will be free of the suffocating grasp that anxiety currently has on your life.

I also want you to know that I completely sympathize with you and that I truly know what you are going through. This book comes straight from my heart to you. It's time for you to learn how to win your life back and to always keep a deep love of life within you. I want you to know that there is an answer, and after going through my own bout with an anxiety disorder, I feel that it is my duty to help others overcome it, too. That means you.

I would also like to make it clear that the purpose of this book is not to help you "cope" with anxiety, as most other books in this genre would have you do. This book is aimed dead-on at your well being and returning you to your normal self. That's all there is to it. Stand fast in the face of your fears and know that your mind is your treasure, your gem, your kingdom to love and protect. Anxiety doesn't belong there. You know that.

I also promise not to sugarcoat anything here. This is not going to be easy. The road ahead is a bumpy one, though the actual steps are totally simple and very easy to perform. But what you are going to have to experience in terms of mental discomfort will not be easy. And you have to realize that you must do this alone.

You are the only one who can think and feel *the things that you think and feel.* Unless someone has experienced anxiety before, they will never even begin to comprehend how you are feeling. I know that what you are going through seems to be Hell right now, but the only way you will be well is to trust and believe in this book and more importantly, yourself.

This may not be easy for you and I understand that, but this is the only way. You must be brave. Face yourself and your anxiety. You will come out a stronger *you* after this is all over, and you will be satisfied with the fact that sweet victory was yours because you were able to attain it all on your own.

How does that sound? You know that the time to get rid of it is now. *You have anxiety. It does not have you.*

Remember that. However clichéd those words may sound, they are true nonetheless. This is your time. This is where you have to face yourself. And believe it or not, you can choose to use anxiety to make you or to break you mentally. Make your choice now.

THE ANATOMY OF ANXIETY

In order for you to truly learn how to become well again, it is important that you understand the make-up of anxiety and to realize what causes it. Essentially your brain is working in a fundamentally normal fashion, but it's a bit out of order. What this means is that it's okay to feel anxious or scared at times. Anxious or fearful feelings are natural, but when they arrive at inappropriate times — as tends to be the case with an anxiety disorder — this is when the "out-of-order" sign gets posted. This is when a red flag is raised up and something must be done.

Here is how I have come to understand it. The word 'anxiety' simply refers to a state of worry.

In the case of people who suffer with an anxiety disorder, they find themselves to be in a habitual, excessive, and possibly even a perpetual state of worry. In other words, when someone has anxiety, the worry stays for quite some time and the level of worry tends to be high.

This might be a tough pill to swallow, but you must understand that it is entirely true. We are the cause of anxiety and its symptoms. It is our own minds that cause us to feel this way. It's not our parents, our kids, work, school, our in-laws, or anything else. We can't point our fingers anywhere other than at the reflection in the mirror. Come to terms with this immediately.

People may have told you that something outside of you causes you to feel anxious. This is not the case. You are the only one in control of your mind, the only one who causes you to feel the way that you feel. Keep reading and you'll find out why.

I had to realize the same thing. It will actually make you feel better because once you accept this it will help you fully realize that you are not mentally ill, and this realization will empower you to take the reins and move forward.

When you feel anxious, it is because you are simply overanalyzing things. When you overanalyze things, you try to come up with an explanation for everything, and when you do this, you try to clarify your anxious feelings, *and when you can't, you panic.*

You probably end up thinking, "Oh! I must have a mental illness!" or "Oh my God! I'm dying," when in all reality, you are fine. Since you're over thinking these ideas and coming up with crazy scenarios in your mind, they feel completely true and real. This is usually when thoughts of the things that frighten you the most come about.

Another thing people tend to do when feeling anxious about a certain idea, object, or situation is that they avoid it completely. This is a serious issue, because when you feel anxious and begin to avoid those things that make you feel that way, you allow the anxiety to dictate your life more and more. And as you do, you form fearful habits. It all snowballs until you eventually can't leave the house because you are so scared.

Of course, you logically tell yourself and logically *know* that there isn't a single thing to be afraid of. You know that there's nothing to harm you at work or in a dark room at night. But because of these deep and strong feelings, you believe that it must be true.

Logic tells you that you were fine for the period of time before you felt anxious. Yet you *feel* as though you could be mentally ill, and nothing can invoke those deep feelings of fear of mental illness unless they are true, right? Wrong.

Whatever you feel can be traced back to one person. You. You are the only one who can have control of your feelings.

This next bit may sound a bit harsh so brace yourself.

You are totally and completely obsessed with yourself. You are obsessed with the way things make you feel and how bad those feelings are when they arrive. Nothing matters more to you when you feel anxious than *you* and the way you feel.

This might be something that you hate to hear at a time like this, but you must understand right now that what I'm telling you is a hundred percent true.

Think about it. Where do your anxious thoughts come from? You. Where do your feelings come from? You. Where do those palpitations, cold clammy hands, and dizziness come from? You. Your thoughts, feelings, and symptoms come from you and your personal beliefs. They do not come from other people, places, things, or anything else outside of yourself.

I want you to know right now that you are not mentally ill in any way shape or form, although it may seem that way to you presently. If you were indeed mentally ill or psychotic, you would think that you were fine. In other words, you wouldn't know you were psychotic or that you were behaving any differently. Psychotic people are in a state where they have absolutely zero sense of reality. You therefore wouldn't realize that you were out of your norm.

You obviously have some sense of reality, because you wouldn't be looking for a solution or be reading this book, and you wouldn't realize that you weren't functioning normally. Think about that.

Do psychotic people ask themselves if they are psychotic? Do they seek help on their own, in the way that you are now? Do psychotic people try to make sense of anything inside or outside of themselves? Of course not. They do none of the above. They don't even notice.

A person with a mental illness has no idea that they are mentally ill in most cases. Having said that, you can rest assured that anxiety is not a psychotic disorder. It is incorrect to put it in the same category as psychological infirmity. It is a disorder, yes, but it is a disorder in the sense that it is simply a state of the mind being out of order, which then needs to be put *back* in order, much in the same way one reorganizes files in a portfolio or on a computer.

Anxiety is a learned behavior. That's right, you have *learned* to be this way, much in the same way you learned how to swim or ride a bike when you were a child. When you ride a bike you don't think much about it, you just ride the bike.

It doesn't necessarily matter what or who taught you to be this way. It is simply that you have not been able to appropriately handle certain reactions to fears that you had following a certain experience.

Your mind was bombarded with things it couldn't handle at some point, and you eventually developed an anxious condition. Now, more often than not, anxiety is driven by being overly concerned or worried about anything that comes your way. It could be about one thing or a group of things. A lot of the time, the concern is based upon the unknown.

A person with an anxiety disorder is constantly afraid of what *could* happen. It's the *possibility* that the anxious person focuses their concentration on. They are always trying to expect a highly unpleasant yet equally unlikely event, trying to plan for a future misgiving in an effort to avoid it or start coping with it beforehand.

They paint scenarios in their minds that start off bad, and then end up growing into far worse events. Maybe this sounds familiar: You think of what might happen, causing this to happen, causing that to happen, after that happens, then this will do that, and this will occur, and then finally — *now wait a sec!* Stop and think about all of this.

First of all, do you realize that the first thing hasn't even happened? It never does happen, does it? Think about that. I'm sure you have experienced this train of thought before. The condition of constant anxiety develops when you start making an effort to avoid anything and everything that makes you feel anxious or discomforted in any way, because you don't feel that you can handle it. It's a defense mechanism.

You are unconsciously trying to protect yourself from things you unconsciously perceive as dodgy or dangerous. Obviously, there is nothing really unsafe happening to you. There is no tiger in the shrubs stalking you nor a car coming at you head on as you cross the street. It's just that you have learned to seek *comfort through constantly avoiding discomfort.*

What you need to realize is that constantly avoiding discomfort does not make it go away. Another thing that you need to know about discomfort is that that's all it is. Discomfort. It's just a feeling, and it's neither bad nor good. It just is.

You may know this already, but there are glands sitting above your kidneys called *adrenal glands.* These glands secrete a hormone called, you guessed it, *adrenaline.* Adrenaline is used to help you survive in a dangerous situation, giving you a high but temporary boost in strength, pain tolerance, vision, and speed of movement.

It triggers what is known as the "fight or flight" response, which basically means what the name implies. You will either fight the danger presented to you or flee from it. We observe animals exhibiting this all of the time on nature programs. As a cheetah darts after a gazelle, the gazelle will naturally run away to avoid being eaten.

What you are feeling when you feel anxious are the effects of the "fight or flight" response; the basic feeling of adrenaline. The difference between normal people, animals, and anxious people, is that anxious people have learned to be afraid to feel the fight or flight response after being exposed to it, and handling it improperly on a consistent basis.

Normally, adrenaline is released when you are in real danger. It goes to your muscles to help you fight or run and numbs your body to any pain. Your eyes dilate so you can see extraordinarily well. Adrenaline is really your friend and it was given to us to help us survive.

The problem is that you are afraid of adrenaline and its effects without realizing it. Adrenaline is usually released in a situation where your body is in danger, and it is truly there to help you save yourself and survive a dangerous ordeal. In normal cases, the effects of adrenaline wear off as the adrenal glands discontinue secreting adrenaline, and you feel back to normal again.

It's all in the name of survival. However, you must remember that you are a human being and unlike the members of the animal kingdom, you have the ability to think consciously for yourself. And having such an ability you are able to study and change yourself, rather than operate on instinct alone.

However, in the case of anxiety, adrenaline is released inappropriately, causing you to feel the way you do. What follows is your withdrawal from what you perceive to be dangerous. So in a sense, anxiety is normally there to protect you. It's there to help you survive a truly hazardous state of affairs thereby avoiding danger.

Now, however, the adrenal glands respond to your reaction to discomfort by saying, "Well hey, if you're feeling so terrible, you have to be in danger. You need more adrenaline!" And as you receive more adrenaline, you continue to feel scared, and then you receive *more adrenaline.*

This can cause people to really freeze up, because they mistake adrenaline for the words *I'm scared*, and you continue to tell yourself this until you leave the party, or quit your job, or avoid whatever is causing you to worry or feel uneasy.

The purpose of adrenaline is simple. It is there to cause you to withdraw from or fight in a condition that is risky or too dangerous.

In normal cases, you would have felt the feelings for a little while, and you would soon feel back to normal. Now, however, your anxiety is stuck in place, causing you to feel this way for most if not all the time. This is because you have created the *habit* of anxious behavior, breeding the *habit* of releasing adrenaline, causing you to almost always feel shaky, dizzy, etc.

The habit is formed in the same way you create the habit of turning the light on when you enter a room or closing the door on your way out of the house. After doing it time and again, it happens without your conscious thought. You experience discomfort in a situation every time you are exposed to it, remember that discomfort, and experience it every time you are met with that situation or object again.

People normally mistake the feeling of adrenaline for fear, causing them to start what I like to call the "Fear Cycle".

The way it works is pretty simple. You have a mind. There are two parts to it, known as the *conscious* mind and *subconscious* mind. The conscious side is the one you are aware of at any given time. You mostly use it to accept or reject ideas after giving them your conscious attention.

Habits are formed in the subconscious side of your mind. This side of your mind is the one that you are totally unaware of. The subconscious can only accept what the conscious mind continues to give it. It only says, "Yes." Your subconscious mind begins to form a fearful habit when you constantly give it your frightful thoughts towards certain experiences.

Whatever you give the subconscious mind, it can only say, "Yes." *I'm scared.* "Yes." *This is terrible.* "Yes." *This makes me feel frightened.* "Yes." *I can't deal with this.* "Yes." *I'm scared.* You get the idea.

When you do something regularly, you create a habit and cease thinking about it as you do it. It happens automatically. The same holds true here. When you react to the sensations of adrenaline improperly on a regular basis, you create a habit. This habit is what you know as anxiety.

Again, the subconscious only accepts the ideas you hand it. Since it only accepts those ideas, it thinks that your everyday experiences and all of the anxiety associated with these occurrences as *normal,* because of how often it all happens, and because of how often you continue to fear things.

That's why your anxious feelings occur all of the time — simply because of old *bad habits.* Now, as you think about this condition *consciously,* you know logically that being anxious all of the time isn't normal. However, in your *subconscious* mind, it's completely normal.

Again, the difference between your *conscious mind* and your *subconscious mind* is that your *conscious mind* is the one you can control. It is the side of your mind that you can tell to accept or reject ideas. Your conscious mind is the part that you are *aware* of when you think about or do things.

You can't control your subconscious mind consciously. What I mean by this is that you can't tell it to think something the same way you would with your conscious mind. For example, you can tell your conscious mind to think of a pink hippo, and you would instantly create that picture in your head.

However, you can't simply think "no more anxiety" to change what's going on within your subconscious mind. That takes *action*.

When I was going through anxiety, I did a ton of research on the brain. Getting slightly scientific, there is an organ in your brain called the Hippocampus, an organ comprised of two curved finger-like appendages in the brain.

The Amygdala (uh-mig-duh-luh) is an almond shaped organ at the tip of each "finger" of the Hippocampus, and is involved with setting the standard, or "benchmark" if you will, for your emotional reactions.

Certain environmental factors, or stimuli, may cause you to act in a certain way. As you react to certain stimuli in certain ways over and over again, the Amygdala remembers these reactions, causing you to form those habits, and therefore triggering those reactions any time those stimuli enter your environment.

It will associate those objects with your feelings of fear and anxiety, causing you to become anxious whenever you are met with them. For example, if you feel anxious every time you try to leave the house, it is because you have made a habit of being afraid every time you go to leave the house. Your Amygdala remembers this reaction and now sees it as, "If I leave the house, I will be in danger," and your fears persist, although you know that there is no danger present.

This leads to a lot of discomfort so you may stop leaving the house altogether. In short, you have habituated anxious behavior.

Your mind has decided that these fearful behaviors are your normal and appropriate habits, thus you continue to experience anxiety.

Remember when you rode your bike on your training wheels way back when? Once you pushed on the pedals correctly and rode the bike many times, the training wheels came off right? You then rode that cute little bike on two wheels without even thinking about it consciously. You just did it.

The same principle applies here. Your training wheels in this case are your first **conscious reactions** to your anxious sensations and feelings. When you react the same way enough times to your anxious feelings, the training wheels (your consciously controlled reactions) come off, and you ride your "bike of anxiety" so to speak on two wheels without thinking about it.

So you're anxious at an unconscious level. You do it out of habit, without thinking about it consciously. You just do it. To be well, you simply have to learn how to ride the "anxiety-free bike," the bike of wellness. This book will instruct you how to put that bike together and ride it. Then eventually you can build the habit of non-anxious behavior, and take the training wheels off.

You will habituate non-anxious behavior (normal and appropriate behavior) and you will no longer have to think about it as you behave this way. Essentially, you are cutting the habit of anxious behavior and replacing it with the habit of normal behavior.

Whether someone's anxiety manifests itself as shyness, fearfulness, social anxiety, or depersonalization (as in my case), they are all one and the same in that they are signs of an underlying anxiety disorder that needs to be taken care of.

BELIEFS

Everything starts somewhere, and your thoughts are no exception. You already know that your thoughts begin with you, but have you ever taken the time to think about where those thoughts (including those associated with fear and anxiety) begin? It's a mind-boggling idea. Where do our thoughts come from? You may say the subconscious mind. That's partly true, but the subconscious mind isn't the first place where thoughts are initiated. It goes a bit deeper than that. One word: Beliefs.

The fearful belief systems that are deeply set in your subconscious mind will ultimately decide how you think, feel, and act. You have formed or have grown up with those beliefs, whether you realize it or not.

We all have certain beliefs that specific things in the world are scary. Certain things must be intimidating or frightening to us, and this happens because we were raised with those beliefs or developed them through our experiences. There is a belief behind every fear that you have. The first belief is that something has to scare you to begin with. Why does that particular object of fear bother you in the first place? Whenever you come across a fear, start breaking it down and ask yourself these questions:

- What am I afraid of?
- What can result from encountering that object?
- Am I in mortal danger?
- If not, why am I scared?
- What exactly am I feeling right now?

When you answer those questions, don't think too hard about them. Answer them honestly and completely. When you do, you will quickly realize that your fear only exists because you created it in your mind. Your mind is a very powerful thing, and when you use it to create something like fear towards an object, and do it on a continuous basis, you will always be afraid.

What you need to do is break down your fears. Get out a pen and paper and write out all of your fears. Now beneath each fear, ask yourself the questions above and answer them fully and honestly.

Have you ever wondered how or why we perceive things the way we do? Have you ever asked yourself why things annoy us, scare us, make us angry, make us sad, or even how they make us feel in general? What is it about certain things that make people joyful or not?

People react differently to certain things they experience in life, and here's why: It's because of us. It's because of our beliefs that shape the way we walk, talk, and go about our business and affairs throughout our lives. *How can that be?* It's simple really.

Have you noticed how some things might scare the hell out of one person but then be absolutely invigorating to another? Or how something might annoy someone but be hilarious to someone else? We have all witnessed this in some form or another.

Imagine someone tells a fairly vulgar joke to one of their friends, and they bust their guts laughing. But then, when they tell someone else the same exact joke, the recipient ends up being offended in some way. Hold on a sec. How can that be possible? Jokes are supposed to be funny, so why would someone be offended? The joke teller didn't say anything different, but the reaction received from the two different people were on opposite ends of the spectrum.

Here's another example. Say someone is deathly afraid of heights. They probably feel terrified of things like flying, roller coasters, or standing atop skyscrapers or towers. This person is horrified at the thought of heights and can barely ride an airplane in a collected state of mind. How is it possible, then, that someone can jump out of that same plane, fall towards the ground at over 300 miles per hour and enjoy it?

It's all a matter of how we perceive things; how we follow and practice our beliefs. And the "how" is developed as we are raised and exposed to certain events over the course of our lives, and as we develop our belief systems.

As stated in an earlier chapter, you have learned how certain things in life should affect you from others. However, it isn't really what you were exposed to or how mommy and daddy brought you up that formed your perception of life. It ultimately comes down to how you have learned to *react* to certain things in your life.

I say that these reactions were learned because they were other people's reactions first. Think about it. You probably watched your parents' reactions as they saw or experienced things that scared them. In a child's mind, what a parent does is right. So as you watched your parents — or even other people — react to certain things with fear, you decided that that is an appropriate reaction, *whether you decided this consciously or unconsciously.*

We all have certain beliefs about life, and those very same beliefs apply to fears that we may have. Somewhere inside of you, you believe that certain things are *supposed* to be frightening, whether those things are associated with your anxiety disorder or otherwise.

Consider this next example. Almost everyone's been raised with the idea that sharks are to be feared just like in the *Jaws* movies.

When many people think of sharks, they think of a big, muscular, demonically proportioned monster of death and doom swimming swiftly towards its victim, it's menacing dorsal fin visible on the water's surface.

The victim, whether a human or an animal, is trying to swim away in a futile attempt to evade the shark. Then, as the creepy music becomes more intense, a view of the shark's huge pink jaw comes into view as it juts out of its mouth, exposing its terrifyingly huge and serrated pearly whites.

Finally, the victim is pulled under with an almost supernatural force. As the victim quickly descends below the ocean's surface, they disappear from view, and the water is stained a deep red.

That is what a lot of people think of when the word "shark" comes to mind. Yet, in spite of all of this, we can sit down in front of a television or aquarium and watch as divers swim with those same exact creatures. The divers feed the sharks, film them, and even pet them! How is this possible? How can they love being down there with those big, bad, man-eating monsters from Hell?

What makes them different from those who have a fear of sharks? They have simply learned to get over the widespread and blindly fearful beliefs towards sharks by learning about them, facing them eye-to-eye, respecting them, and even expressing love and admiration for them. This fear, along with any other fear known to man, can be conquered.

Let's think about this next statement. Take it in with an open mind, and appreciate its truth. Your mind is absolutely brilliant. Now you probably didn't expect that, did you? Well in all honesty, I am not just saying that, because it really is truly incredible when you think about it. Look at what it does.

Your mind takes an idea about a certain fear that you have and rockets off to the moon with it, causing you to completely over think small things. It takes a thought in your head, packs it with tons of gunpowder, and fires it through a cannon! Do you see where I am going with all of this?

You're just thinking way, way, *way,* too hard about insignificant things. They seem relevant to you, but they really aren't, and you have to get a grip on this. For instance, we can use my personal experience as an example. You may get an uncomfortable feeling in your chest. Maybe it's a tight, slightly burning feeling. All of a sudden you start worrying that you are having a heart attack, and actually believe it.

Of course, you aren't really having a heart attack. It could be a bad case of heartburn or a muscle cramp. But since you believe that you are indeed having a heart attack it seems as though you really are, simply because you believe it.

To you, that heart attack is happening and you're living through it. However, there is no heart attack. You are not dying of whatever atrocious disease you're thinking of. Forget about all of that nonsense; it simply isn't there. To say I was relieved when I realized this is an understatement, to say the least. Comprehend right now, at this very moment in your life, that your mind is brilliant. Ponder this for a while. Your mind has so much energy and power. It obviously has to, since it can get you to believe the craziest things, right? It's just that all that power and brilliance is being channeled in the wrong direction. You use your powerful creative and analytical abilities to concentrate on those negative feelings and how badly things must be for you, rather than the great and wonderful things about you that should be truly shining in your mind.

RELAX

Being able to relax may seem like a tough task for those with anxiety, and it may even seem impossible. Let me begin by saying it is completely possible to unwind, get calm, and relax. You may be thinking *Hady, how can I relax when I have ANXIETY! Come on!*

Let me ask you this: Are you anxious *all of the time?* By all of the time I mean *100%* of every hour making up the twenty-four hours of every day? Seriously, are you anxious all of the time? No, of course you aren't. If you were anxious all the time you wouldn't be sitting here reading this book now, would you? When a person has anxiety, they are always trying to find a way to relax.

You are always searching for a way to avoid the anxious feelings, so you may feel at ease.

You are always looking for answers, hoping to find a solution, so you can finally be rid of this anxiety and to finally be able to get a rest from it. That's all you are looking for on a constant basis, whether you realize it or not. I know that's how it was for me.

Relaxation is a very important step to overcoming anxiety once and for all. Anxiety is a state of mind where excessive worry is an everyday thing. You probably worry about things that, to you, may be nothing less than horrible. You may even think that you are dying of some dreaded disease. But you have to put that out of your mind completely, because whatever you think that ailment is, it simply doesn't exist.

The key to this step is to learn to relax instead and let go. This will help you learn to calm your mind down. As you tranquilize your mentality, your worries will slowly diminish, helping you to rid yourself of anxiety. It's also worth noting that relaxation is a part of every other step in this book in one way or another.

When I had anxiety, I figured hey, if I'm always tense and worried, maybe I could learn how to always be relaxed. It seems logical that you should learn how to relax, don't you think? At the very least it gets you headed in the right direction and allows you to have a more positive attitude when you examine your present condition. Not to mention it helps you take it easy a bit, which everyone needs to do these days.

The idea behind this step is that you begin to shift your attention towards a positive and effective effort towards wellness. As you adjust your focus in the proper direction, instead of devoting your concentration to anxiety and its residual problems, you create a mindset that will allow you to be at ease.

Once you are able to relax — at will — in any given moment, you will become well in every sense. Here are a few very simple techniques to help you relax if you ever feel anxious:

Breathing

Our lungs are magnificent organs. They allow us the ability to breathe, the most important act we carry out in order to sustain the life in our bodies. That's right, breathing is the most important thing we do during our physical lifetime.

Think about it. We can survive weeks without food. Eating is an integral part of survival, however we can last a while without it. We can live for days without water. Drinking water keeps our bodies hydrated and operating at its optimum level. However, we can only live for but a few minutes without oxygen. If you couldn't breathe for a minute, you would be in some really serious pain.

If you couldn't breathe for two minutes, you would give everything you have in your possession to be able to breathe again. If you couldn't breathe for three minutes or more, you would be dead. Oxygen in the air allows all of the cells to function. Without oxygen, they wither and die. That's why you must learn how to breathe properly.

In the case of an anxious person, they may not be breathing deeply enough at times. This is a problem because your body won't get enough oxygen, which may cause the symptoms that spark more worry for you, such as palpitations in my case, dizziness due to less oxygen getting to the brain, etc.

It won't kill you, because you're still breathing after all. However, it isn't helping you either, and you must correct your breathing. Breathing can always be improved, much in the same way that a person can learn to write better or improve their driving skills.

When I had an anxiety disorder, I found myself breathing irregularly at times. I would exhale a lot longer than I would inhale, and would all of a sudden find myself breathing in hard *because of my lack of proper breathing.* It seemed like a serious problem at the time, but it really wasn't. All I had to do was simply breathe with a conscious effort to eventually form a habit of breathing properly. When I did this, my palpitations went away. I felt better overall, simply by correcting my breathing.

Whether or not you are short of breath, you must learn to breathe properly. When you breathe, make a conscious effort to breathe *deeply,* and from your belly. A simple exercise to help you relax your breathing is to breathe in for five seconds, and exhale for ten seconds.

As you inhale, breathe the air in through your nose, and when you exhale, breathe out through your mouth.

As you breathe in, don't expand your ribs, but rather put the pressure on your diaphragm, expanding your abdomen. Breathing this way will help you relax and allow you to take in more oxygen, in addition to reducing the amount of respirations you make. Thus you breathe slower.

Proper and slowed breathing can help you relax should you feel a panic attack coming on. Consciously focus on filling your lungs completely. Expand your lungs until they are completely full of air, and you feel there is no room left for any more. Then, exhale nice and slowly. Ideally, you'll want to exhale more slowly than when you inhale.

You will quickly notice how your breathing slows down and how you feel much more relaxed and at ease. This technique can help you achieve a deeply relaxed or even meditative state. You can use this technique to help you reduce your anxiety about something or even use it to help you fall asleep at night.

Meditation

Meditation is used as a ritual by many different religions. Hinduism, Buddhism, Christianity, and Islam are just a few of them. We are all familiar with the cross-legged or sitting position of Hindus and Buddhists, but tribute and prayer are also considered forms of meditation.

Muslims perform five daily prayers and engage in "zikr," or remembrance of God. Christians attend church services. The practice of meditation has many different methods. However, in whatever form it is chosen, it is all around us.

This meditation step is highly effective, because it involves you becoming deeply relaxed, allowing you to put anxiety aside and feel at ease. Meditation is an incredibly excellent way to help you achieve this state of ease. It inspires you to look deeply within your own being; to allow you to get to know and be more comfortable with yourself.

You learn a lot more about the true you inside, things that you may have never even imagined previously. Meditation is very easy and you can do this any time during the day. I preferred to meditate during the night when my family was asleep and I was sure that I wouldn't be disturbed. So let's begin.

Decide what time of day you would like to meditate. Then, find a comfortable and quiet place where you can be alone and at peace. Sit in a position that you feel comfortable in, whether it is sitting up or lying down. Personally I liked to be on my knees, sitting on my heels with a pillow under my insteps.

Now, as you sit comfortably, lay your hands in your lap. You can clasp your hands or interlace your fingers if you like. The key is that you have to be totally comfortable with your position so that you are not distracted by any physical discomfort or pain while you meditate. A big part of meditation is to remain at peace, without any distraction. Once you are comfortable, close your eyes.

All you need to do after that is to focus on breathing as we discussed earlier. Slow your breathing down more and more as time passes. Calm your mind, and by this I mean that you should simply stop thinking. Sounds hard, doesn't it? But it gets easier with practice. You can begin by focusing on only one thing, and blocking everything else out.

Try this. Simply concentrate on your breathing. All you need to think about is your breathing. Focus your mind on your breathing. Now, focus on the rise and fall of your chest and how long your breaths are. Really try to draw a blank in your mind. Set aside your worries and everything else clouding your mind. Let this be your time. Convince yourself that the most important thing at this moment is concentrating on on your breathing.

Now, when you feel that your breathing is nice, slow, calm, and relaxed, imagine something that makes you feel incredibly comfortable, preferably something fluid, like a breeze, wave, or water. Imagine this object of comfort slowly flowing over every area of your body. We'll use water as an example.

Start with your feet and work your way up. Imagine the water flowing around your toes, your arches, and heels of your feet. Feel every fibrous band of tissue in your feet relax as the water flows over them. Now, imagine it working its way up your legs, winding around your shins, knees and thighs. Feel the muscles in your legs relax and release all evidence of tension. Imagine the water now working up your hips and abdominal area, relaxing every muscle within.

Then, imagine it flowing around your chest and arms, deeply relaxing all of the muscles there. Finally, see that water spiraling around your head, relaxing all of the muscles in your face and neck. The idea is to consciously relax every tiny muscle fiber as the object of comfort — water in this case — flows around the area you're relaxing.

The key in this is to use your imagination with commitment in the same way you use it to feel anxious.

Believe what you are imagining. Really use the power of your mind to create this visualization. Take your time and take it slow. Really try to create every second with a committed effort. Channel that same power that you have used to construct those anxious thoughts in your mind towards this powerful relaxation instead.

Keep in mind that this is just an example. You can create any scenario you wish. The point is to really live in these blissful moments while you relax and meditate. See it, feel it, and create all of the images with the boundless power of your mind.

Instead of using the power that you have to foster anxiety in your mind, create this powerfully relaxing scenario instead. After you decide that your body is fully relaxed, count backwards from one thousand, and with every count, imagine yourself sinking into the floor (or wherever you are sitting), sinking with and into total comfort. Envision yourself descending comfortably. You can imagine yourself going down a spiral staircase, and with each count, you take a step down.

Or, you can imagine slowly floating downward in the sky, and with each count, you pass a cloud. With each count really feel yourself sink deeper and deeper into total comfort. As you do this, your body will begin to feel pleasantly tingly and heavy. When you begin to feel this way, you'll know that you are doing it right.

This doesn't have to be a chore. Try and have fun with this, because this can be a great time for you to get to know and become comfortable with yourself. And again, you should do whatever feels right for you, because everyone's different.

Meditation can last anywhere from minutes to hours at a time. You can decide how long you want to do this. When you feel that you are satisfied with your meditation, all you have to do is take a nice deep breath, yawn and stretch if you like, and open your eyes. I will warn you that Meditation can be addictive! The relaxation it brings is absolutely incredible, and it is very satisfying knowing that you are able to do it all on your own.

Meditation is a great way to start or end your day, reduce stress, and just feel better in general. The Zazen meditation of Zen is my personal favorite. All you must do is sit and observe your thoughts. Listen to them, but keep a *detached mind* (explained later). Just watch your thoughts on the screen of your mind, but don't let your feelings get stuck on a certain thought. All you must do is simply observe your thoughts from the outside, without becoming affected by them.

Exercise

Exercising your body provides countless benefits. Increasing your physical health and vitality is a foundation for living a happy and healthy life. As you can probably tell, this is one of my favorite things to do.

Vigorous exercise is a phenomenal way to relieve any stress in your life. Exercise fatigues the body and mind, and afterward you feel pleasantly tired. It will totally divert your mind from any and every problem you may be experiencing. This holds true for those with and without an anxiety disorder.

As you exercise, you release any negative feelings you have within you, such as anger. Cranking out repetitions with heavy weights will effectively allow you to express any negativity within you in a healthy way, and afterward, you'll feel unbelievably satisfied.

This feeling of satisfaction is known as the "Runner's High." Runner's High is the pleasant sensation a person gets after vigorously exercising for a period of time, whether they did so by swimming, running, lifting weights, boxing, cycling, Muay Thai, rowing, or any other activity that involves strenuous activity.

It's caused by an activated release of Endorphins from the Pituitary gland in the brain. The word "endorphin" has its own meaning as well. It comes from the prefix "endo-" meaning "within" and "-orphin" meaning "morphine." Imagine that! We can release a natural and safe equivalent to morphine on our own, simply by exercising!

Morphine is normally used to relieve pain, and our endorphins may be released due to the brain interpreting exercise as pain. Whatever the reason is, that release creates a pleasurable feeling of euphoria, and you'll feel happy immediately after exercising. Runner's High only seems to come about after very hard activity.

I enjoy various types of exercise such as heavy lifting, cardio workouts, and Muay Thai. I like to make that Runner's High my end goal, and I know that once I reach it, I have done a good job. As you exercise and continue to do so on a regular basis, you'll look better, feel better, sleep better, become stronger, and live longer (not to mention you will also enjoy countless mental benefits as well).

Exercising only takes an hour or less, depending on your level of fitness and the intensity of your workout. If you can spend time doing something that doesn't benefit you, such as watching television or moaning about the past, you have time to exercise. You must force yourself out of any laziness that is keeping you from achieving your best.

That's really all it is. Believe me that once you start working out and watching your body change for the better, you will absolutely love every second of it! Exercise can be addicting, but don't worry about that. There are positive and negative addictions. Exercising regularly is a very positive addiction. You'll be able to have a positive impact on your mind and body as you work out. As you exercise, your muscles will grow beautifully, your heart will begin to pump blood more efficiently, your lungs will oxygenate your body with competence, and then, your mind will follow suit.

And there are plenty of exercises that don't require any equipment at all. You can simply walk up and down the stairs in your house, and perform calisthenics such as push-ups or sit-ups. Once again, there really isn't a single valid excuse for not exercising. The values and benefits of keeping your body fit are endless!

Try to devise a workout plan for yourself, and be realistic. Do what feels right for you. You may not like weights. Maybe you just want to run a few blocks or even a couple of miles. That's fine too. Do what feels good and gives you a nice and satisfying 'burn' when you're finished. The burn means it's working!

The mental benefits that come along with working out are great. However, just as you isolate muscles in your workouts, you should also isolate the exercise of your mind as well. You should try to put a separate focus on the development of your mind, because it is just as important as exercising the muscles of your body.

Your mind can be expanded and improved in a plethora of ways. Anything involving deep thought works great. Take these examples for instance. You can read, write, study, learn a new language, or ponder about a deep subject such as the origins of the universe. Think of things that get your thoughts going. Anything that can jog your mind in this manner is a great way to exercise your mind.

Hypnosis

Okay. Expand the mind here. This may sound a bit different or odd, but it works, *if you let it.*

I began using hypnosis for one simple reason. I realized that I believed any anxiety-related thought that crossed my mind, no matter how far-fetched it was. So I decided that if I could do that, maybe I could believe the suggestions offered by hypnosis.

As I found out soon enough, it really does work. The changes in my awareness allowed me to create better mental habits. For example, I learned how to mentally relax, rather than be anxious. I learned how to focus on the solution, rather than the problem. I even learned how to let go of guilt, anger, and sadness. This stuff works. You simply have to allow it in.

Hypnosis can be undertaken in a number of ways. You can visit a hypnotist, or you can do what I did. Thankfully, I had access to the Internet, and was able to download hypnotic audios that allowed me to experience hypnosis on my own. It was nice and very convenient to be able to experience this extraordinary technology in the comfort of my home and deal with this on my own terms without having to visit with a therapist.

I have personally found hypnosis audios to be quite beneficial while I dealt with anxiety. They can be found all over the Internet, available as a free download or for a small fee. Simply play the audio with a pair of headphones, and you're in business. All you have to do is listen. The hypnotist on the recording will guide you through the process. You are simply allowing their suggestions past any conscious resistance into your subconscious mind and accepting them. It's quite a unique experience and I highly recommend it.

Like I said before, expand the mind here. I have found hypnosis audios to be quite relaxing and they really do work if you let them. The hypnotic trance is nothing more than a very pleasant and open state of mind. Your body may feel comfortably heavy and you may feel a tingling sensation throughout your body. You are still conscious, but your mind is open and relaxed.

The key is to **allow** the trance to happen. To do this, simply listen to and focus on the hypnotist and nothing else. As the suggestions are given to your subconscious mind over a period of time, it will accept them, and you will begin to realize the presence of those changes in your day-to-day activities.

Hypnosis is very similar to meditation. The only difference is that there is someone guiding you through it. They help you create the relaxing image in your mind, rather than you doing it yourself as you meditate. They will put you through the same essential steps to achieve a calm, comfortable, and a happily meditative and pleasantly dream-like state.

Once again, the main idea behind this chapter is to relax. I'm sure you have been looking tirelessly for an answer; an end to anxiety. Be pleased to know that your search is over now, and that you have found the answer.

Take a deep breath and unwind because you are not mentally ill, and there is absolutely nothing medically wrong with you because you are simply anxious, not ill.

Anxiety is just another word for being in a state of worry, or nervousness. In a nutshell, you are just really, really, worried and nervous, nothing more, and nothing less.

It is quite simply wrong to place it in the category along with other mental illnesses. Allow yourself to really absorb this right now. Understand and believe that you are in no way shape or form mentally ill. This condition that you are in can be resolved, and through a much more simple method than you might otherwise think.

STEP 2

UNDERSTAND

This step is absolutely crucial. You've learned about the way anxiety works in your brain, but now you have to learn about the feelings themselves. What's the difference, you might ask. The distinction between the two is that you actually feel the feelings and are aware of them consciously. You don't feel what's happening with you anatomically.

Here's an example. Let's say you are on an African safari. As you are enjoying the sights and sounds, a lion comes rocketing towards you, and he's hungry. This would probably frighten you immensely. First of all, you *feel* fear — you don't *think* it. When you *feel* scared of that lion, you probably aren't thinking "my brain has just interpreted the lion as a danger to my safety, and my hypothalamus has just sent a message to my pituitary gland to trigger my adrenal glands to release a shot of adrenaline into my blood stream in order for me to have a quick energy boost to get out of danger!"

You probably didn't know that that's how the process works until you read that sentence. More than likely, the thought would come out as, "Oh my God! There's a Lion! *RUN!*" Then, you would proceed to high tail your rear end out of there, hopefully in a nice 4x4 vehicle.

So let's say that you encounter that thing which scares you most. How do you feel? Anxiety has many different ways to manifest itself within your awareness. Write the feelings you experience (and what they are caused by) on a sheet of paper. Do this now, and return to the book once you have done this.

Anxiety is something that I believe builds over time. People aren't born anxious. In most cases, a little bit of anxiety is fine; things like being nervous before a big event or while doing something new is normal, and it would eventually subside.

The thing with anxiety disorders is that a habit of anxious thought and behavior is created through learning to think and act anxiously as the thinking and acting is done repeatedly.

Most sufferers of an anxiety disorder, whether it is Generalized Anxiety Disorder, Panic Disorder, etc., wonder why it never goes away, and this is why: It is simply because a bad habit has been learned.

Some people also make the mistake holding all of their problems and burdens within themselves, and not allowing them a way to be expressed. As this happens the feelings inside of a person build up and are piled upon each other. These feelings must eventually manifest somehow. When you think of all of the times you probably kept your negative feelings inside of you, you will realize how true this concept is.

Much of the time — for whatever reason — we tend to internalize our thoughts and feelings within, allowing them no means of expression, without realizing what we are doing to ourselves by allowing these negative feelings to build up within us. It's a lot like a champagne bottle that is shaken up. The fluffy froth accumulates, and air pressure inside of the bottle builds, yet the cork still holds it all in.

The cork may look nice and sturdy on the outside, but it is truly under a lot of pressure. All it takes is a little bit of "help." So once the cork is loosened a bit, it shoots out with enough force to knock someone's teeth out, and the lovely white fizz pours everywhere.

Now if the cork were loosened *before* the champagne bottle was shaken, the fizz would have oozed out sooner, and much less violently. When you don't allow yourself to somehow release what is going on *inside* of you it will eventually manifest itself *outside* of you in its own way.

Anxiety is the end result of an abundant accumulation of repression and worry over a long period of time, which has now manifested itself as habitual worry.

Let's return to those feelings and sensations you wrote down earlier. Now that you have your feelings on that paper, read them aloud, and really become acquainted with them. You may even begin to feel them inside of you. Whatever the case, you need to know one important thing: the feelings that you have associated with your anxiety mean absolutely *nothing*.

Once again, they mean completely nothing. Wrap your head around this right now. The only reason your feelings have so much power and effect on the way you feel, is because *you* give them that power.

You see, as you give those feelings merit, as you visit therapist after therapist, as you give those feelings thought and lose sleep over them, and as you give them more and more attention, you make them stronger.

I gave my anxiety an absolutely ridiculous amount of attention. I was online looking for answers and constantly trying to find an explanation for what was going on, even trying figure out whether I was mentally ill. The simple act of holding onto the feeling, thinking about it constantly as I searched for an answer, and giving it a name, caused it to really stay put. That's how my own anxiety manifested itself.

Depersonalization was the main way anxiety showed itself to me, along with feelings of excessive worry, nervousness, uneasiness, etc. The very fact that I found its name — "Depersonalization" — allowed it to really get locked in place with a nice pedestal to stand firm on.

As a child I could have been just sitting in the car with my father at the wheel or walking around the block with my mom, and this strange feeling would come about. I would think to myself, *I feel like I'm not here. Huh. Weird.* Then I'd simply let go of it and forget about it, and I would feel normal again very soon after.

However, as adults—especially as anxious adults—we tend to blow things ridiculously out of proportion and for whatever reason, the worst outcome is always the most likely outcome in our minds.

We are always trying to explain things, especially when they can't be explained. We try so hard to figure out what's wrong instead of just letting go and letting the situation handle itself. Then when we can't figure it out, we end up feeling guilty or ashamed because we just don't know what to do, or even wind up feeling more scared.

Over analyzing things when you have anxiety is a problem because it is creating fear after fear when you can't figure out what's wrong, and you tend to paint outrageous scenarios in your head, and then *believe them,* causing even more fear. It can really spiral out of control.

When a person has anxiety, they are simply in a state of excessive worry, for little or no reason. The "Fear Cycle" occurs when you feel anxious towards something, acknowledge that feeling, let it affect the way you think and feel, and then become more anxious towards those changes you feel.

The fear cycle is a byproduct of your conscious effort to avoid anxiety. When people are scared of something or associate a negative feeling with it, they naturally try to avoid feeling it again. It's a defense mechanism. People as well as animals naturally avoid things that make them feel bad. Since you try hard to avoid the feelings, you begin to get scared if they begin to settle in, causing more anxiety to occur, causing more fear to occur, followed up by more anxious symptoms.

Remember, anxiety breeds more anxiety. This is an important concept to understand. What happens is that you become scared, you feel those symptoms or feelings, they cause you to become more scared, you create even more symptoms and feelings, you become even more scared, and so on.

When this happens, you will end up trying to avoid what started the fear cycle. However, anxiety can be traced back to one main cause. You.

You are the cause. You must understand this because when I realized this, I overcame my anxiety. You cause your anxiety. This cannot be stressed enough. You have to accept responsibility for the way you think, feel, and act, because you are the only one doing those things.

The main thing you need to understand is that you need not give your anxious thoughts, feelings, and sensations any merit or credibility. Again, that's where anxiety's power comes from — which is the power that you hand right over to it. Anxiety is content to lie back comfortably in a hammock at the beach of your mind. You're doing it without realizing it, and it's not your fault.

You simply need to re-learn normal and appropriate behavior. Tell yourself the truth: *They're just sensations. Just little tingles. There's nothing to worry about. No big deal.*

This really works. Recognizing your anxious feelings as mere sensations, and only regarding them as such, will help you understand what's going on (and you'll relax a bit). It helps you change the way you look at your anxiety and how you feel about it. The idea behind this is simple. Changing your view of how you feel from negative to positive will allow you to cancel out your fears. If you regard these feelings as mere sensations, you can completely shift your attitude in a proper direction.

What exactly are you afraid of? Is it the stimulus, or the thing that you encounter that scares you? Or is it the anxiety, or the scary feeling that you feel? Think about that. When I came to the realization that it was the *feeling* that scared me, and not the actual 'thing' that I saw or heard in front of me, I began to feel better immediately.

The awful **feelings and sensations** a person deals with whenever they are in a fearful situation are what really matter to people. This is what every single solitary fear comes down to. The feelings and sensations are what you truly are afraid of.

If you could stand at the top of a building and feel as though you are standing on a pebble, would you still be afraid? Of course not. That unpleasant feeling that you have comes from the thought of falling. That is what you are truly afraid of. This was a startling discovery for me when I found this out. I realized it when I thought about money.

Everyone says they want more money. They want millions of dollars in their bank accounts. But the thing is, people don't really want money. What is money but fancy paper? What they truly want are the things they can buy with money. But then again, what are cars but fast metal, and what are mansions but much bigger versions of an ordinary house.

It's not the objects of one's desire that one is after. This leaves us with the last part — feelings.

Every want and fear comes down to this. When people pursue things, what they truly want are the feelings of satisfaction and happiness when obtaining ownership of those things. So then it clicked. I thought:

Hey! Fear works exactly the same way! It's not the object of one's fear, but the result of the encounter. Yet it's not really the result, but the feeling of discomfort associated with the thought of that result!

Returning to the shark example, what is the shark, but a big fish with sharp teeth? It has muscles, a cartilaginous skeleton, eyes, gills, etc. It's just an organism, a living thing. You may think otherwise at first, but you aren't afraid of the shark. You may think the fear is based on being bitten by that shark, but that's still not true.

What you are afraid of are the discomforting feelings that you associate with sharks; namely those feelings of fright and terror. Think about it. If one could look at a shark the same way they look at a cute little kitty-cat, would they still be afraid of being in the water with a Great White? Of course not. Sure, they may get killed, but they won't be afraid.

The only reason our sense of fear exists is to keep us alive. It all made sense to me the moment I realized our fears are the same as our wants for happiness and enjoyment, and in that moment I understood that all fears are surmountable. Once you transcend and rise above the unpleasant feelings, you will get over the fear every single time, no matter what it is. This truly is a mind boggling concept.

It's all about how you look at things, and if you can begin to realize that the *feelings* are what scare you, and not the object itself, I absolutely guarantee that you will begin to feel better.

One day I felt like I was going to have a panic attack, and I thought *you know what? Today's the day I fight this. Right Now. If this is going to kill me, I'm gonna go out with a bang.*

Now obviously I was being completely silly. Still, I fought the feelings and I just let them get stronger and stronger, and began to realize that I was the one making them stronger, because I *wanted* them to be, and I wanted them to be stronger since I was telling them to "bring it on" because I wanted to fight them!

I thought fighting it would make it go away, but it just got more and more powerful. Then, I realized that in the end, I was in control of all this! Crazy isn't it?

I felt like an idiot at first. Afterward however, I was ecstatic because I just figured out what the cause of the panic attacks was! Don't be afraid of your feelings. That's what gets people suffering with anxiety truly stuck in their situation. They feel the anxious feelings and get even more scared because of the discomfort that it causes them.

Remember, you aren't exactly scared of that 'thing' that causes you to be frightened or fearful. For example, if someone is afraid of speaking publicly, that's his or her own anxiety manifested as the person's fear of public speaking. It's not the public speaking that scares the person; it's the *discomfort* and unpleasant *feelings* present in those moments.

Another example could involve being in a social situation. Say you get invited to a party, and for some reason you get anxious instead of excited. You feel uncomfortable with the idea of being around all of those people, or what they might think of you. You know in your mind that parties are supposed to be fun, and everyone will be happy to see you. What could be better than friends getting together for a great night?

You may think that you are uncomfortable with being at that party, but in fact what you're afraid of is the *discomfort* you feel borne of your own insecurities whenever you are at a party.

This chain of discomfort and fear might start the fear cycle. There is a simple and easy way to break the fear cycle or stop it from even occurring. All you have to do is **relax.** Don't be afraid of the feelings. Walk casually right into them. Get comfortable there. Laugh at the anxious feelings. Don't fight them, because if you do, you acknowledge their existence, and give them power. Just get into them, and relax. It's as simple as that.

This realization that I was afraid of the negative *feelings and discomfort* associated with what made me feel anxious, rather than the thing itself, was what really got me on the road to wellness. I can't stress enough the power of this realization. With this knowledge, you can, not only conquer your anxiety, but also every fear imaginable. If you can learn to get comfortable with the uncomfortable sensations, you will undeniably be well, because the discomfort is what you interpret *as fear.* If you can let go of the attachment to the discomfort, **voila! — there's no fear, and that 'thing' isn't so scary anymore.**

What you want to do is extract the power from those anxious feelings and use it towards something useful. You may, however, start to feel panic or some other anxious feelings. Don't succumb. Relax into it. Think about something else besides what you are feeling. Talk to a friend about something other than anxiety and how it makes you feel. This may sound frightening at first but this truly works. Ignore the feelings.

If you can't ignore the feelings now, simply acknowledge them, feel them, and really become acquainted with them. Then just let them flow through you without affecting you. This is the key to you becoming well.

Think to yourself as you feel these feelings, *Hey! This isn't so bad after all! These are just feelings and sensations! They don't mean a thing!*

Laugh out loud if you want to! It'll begin to sound funny once you start to understand that anxiety means nothing. I used to laugh at myself all the time. I'd think *Wow! All this time I was so scared of absolutely nothing! Hilarious!*

Have a sense of humor with this. Humor really helps when dealing with your anxiety, or any other less than appealing situation for that matter. Remember that under normal conditions, you would only feel these feelings if you were in some kind of dangerous situation. But what you must realize is that there is no danger present. You have to convince yourself that there isn't a damned thing to be afraid of, whether you are at work, school, the grocery store, the gas station, or in the safety and comfort of your own home.

I completely admit that I was afraid of these anxious feelings, and when I would feel them it made me feel scared, causing them to become even worse. I have experienced the fear cycle. It's no fun and I know that, but you must grasp the fact that the feelings you are having are empty. They truly have zero credibility, and they don't benefit you whatsoever. Remember, anxiety only has the power that you give to it.

- Anxiety is caused by you, you, and only you. Take responsibility.

- Your anxious feelings only exist because you allow them to exist.

- The fear cycle occurs when you learn to become afraid of the anxious feelings.

- When you experience the fear cycle, it is because you are afraid of and trying to avoid the anxious feelings.

- Learn to accept your anxious feelings.

- Feel the anxious sensations, really become acquainted with them, but don't worry or feel afraid of them. Let them flow through your mind without affecting you.

- When you are feeling anxious, you are feeling fear towards nothing.

- As you understand that you are afraid of absolutely nothing, your anxiety will begin to subside.
- It isn't the stimulus that scares you, but the feelings.

- If you think you are about to have a panic attack, don't be afraid. Relax and get into it. Let it get as bad as it can be, and you will realize your true power and control over your anxiety!

ME, ME, ME!

The third step to wellness is what I like to call "Me, Me, Me!" This step is designed to point you in the right direction towards your well being. This involves two things:

1. Learning to cut out your obsession with your condition and how it makes you feel.

2. Learning to give to and love *yourself.*

It seems like a paradox, right? It seems like a contradictory statement: You want to stop self-obsessing, but love yourself at the same time. You might

75

be thinking *well, what's the difference?* I'll tell you. It is pretty negative to be truly obsessed, and have your mind totally occupied with yourself. This is the case with anxiety.

Your day consists of contemplating how you are going to make it through while accommodating your anxiety and preparing for the worst. You worry about the day ahead, instead of being excited about what is to come. You may even feel alone and feel like no one cares. It feels as though you just barely drag by to survive and that you struggle to merely exist.

As you do this, you form anxious habits, dooming yourself to being stuck in a constant state of anxiety. However, it is a totally different story if you can learn to have true, healthy, and deep love and respect for yourself. You deserve love from yourself. When you can truly love yourself, you will be able to tend to your own needs, rather than those of your anxiety.

There are many simple ways to show love to yourself, and some of these are identical to the way that people regularly demonstrate love to others. It can be a truly incredible and rewarding experience to get to know yourself better in these ways. People are always trying to look for things outside of themselves to make them feel better, when in truth they must look *inside*.

You'd be surprised by how little you know about yourself. People tend to be overly concerned with what's going on around them and begin to lose sight of themselves and their own needs, afraid of being selfish or egotistical. Realize now that it is not selfish in any way to love and respect yourself. No one is ever truly happy until they can complete themselves, rather than seeking completion through others. Here are a few simple steps you can take right now to create a feeling of love and respect toward yourself:

Write a letter of gratitude to yourself

Write yourself a letter describing what you are grateful for. Sit down and take an hour or two if you have to. Think of all the things about yourself that you are thankful for. It could be, for example, that you have the hands to hold that paper and pen and write that letter!

You're breathing aren't you? You still have the ability to think coherently enough to read this book, right? Think about that deeper kind of gratitude. Think of all of the different things that you are grateful for, no matter how big or small they are. The roof over your head, the nourishing food you eat, the brain that you think with, the lungs that fill your blood with oxygen, the heart that pumps that blood, your family. You get the idea. You can come up with much more I am sure.

Now think of what makes you, *you*. Just think of the things that make you special. Think of things that you are grateful for. Don't say, "I'm not special," because everyone is in some way. I can prove to you right now that you are. Human beings are like beautiful and ornate handmade jewelry. Every single piece is unique and irreplaceable. You are the same. Unique. Irreplaceable. Think about it. There is only ONE of you in this world. Your fingerprint is unique to you. Every

Human being on earth is special. Just because of the fact that you may not feel loving towards yourself right now doesn't negate the fact you are indeed a very special and deserving person. You can start by giving that letter a title:

- My gratitude list...
- I'm thankful for...
- Thank you for...
- I am so grateful because I...

Play with this step a bit and see what works for you. After you come up with a title, you can then start writing the letter or list. If you choose to write a gratitude letter, start with a greeting in the same way you would write to someone you love and you can begin the body with things such as:

I'm thankful for how you...
I feel great because of...
I love how you...

Anything and everything around you can be appreciated with a feeling of gratitude. Don't limit yourself to the examples given here. You can come up with a bazillion more ways to write this letter. You don't even have to write it as a letter. It could be in the form of a list, an outline, a graphic organizer, or even a PowerPoint presentation if that's what's up your alley.

Do whatever makes you feel good and then convey the message of gratitude towards yourself and the world around you.

Smile

Look in the bathroom mirror every morning and learn to smile at yourself. You probably know how to frown at yourself extremely well, right? Use the same energy that you put behind frowning at yourself to smile at yourself instead.

Look at yourself the same way you would look at a newborn baby. Take in your features. Appreciate them. Love them. Love you. Talk to yourself if you have to. Say to yourself, "I love you, (your name). You are the best. You are meant to be happy. I love you."

Really play with this step. Pretend you are talking to someone that you love. Insert your own little phrases and really try and get creative with this! This may seem odd or even slightly conceited at first. But do you really expect to be able to love others if you can't even love yourself? How do you expect others to love you if *you* don't even love you?

Love yourself first, and then your love for and from others will come and grow. Make it a habit to smile. Smile at your family, your friends, your coworkers, in fact, smile at everyone you meet. Greet people warmly, and make happiness a habit.

Be assertive

Don't be afraid to ask for what you want. If you feel like you have needs that must be met, then meet them. This is a human right. There is nothing wrong with asking for what you want. I'm sure you've experienced times when you wanted to say or do something but you kept silent.

Assertiveness is practiced all around you. You see other people do it all the time. Business executives, car salesman, and doctors practice assertiveness. Even children are assertive when it comes to having their needs met. Of course, I'm suggesting that you assert your requests as a mature adult. Use calm, but firm language when making your requests. Repeat yourself if you have to. Everyone is assertive, and you can be, too. Go ahead and be assertive.

Let go of guilt

This is one of the most important steps. If you choose one step to follow, this is the one. Guilt is a powerful feeling that causes you to lose love for yourself, and it makes you feel low. The first thing to realize is that the past is gone, and it is never, ever going to come back. There is no sense in hanging on to painful memories.

You are the only one who can control your mind. The only reason you may feel guilty is because you continue to allow the memory of that past mistake to exist in your mind. Forget it about it. Don't beat yourself up over mistakes that you made in the past, mistakes you make in the present, or mistakes you think you are going to make in the future. This contradicts what you're trying to do right now, which is to get well.

Let go of any kind of guilt. If you begin to feel guilt creeping up inside of you, recognize it, acknowledge it, and release it. Just let it go. Don't think about it at all. Just let it go.

You must learn to forgive yourself and let go of whatever is in your past that triggers such guilt and shame. Learn to concentrate on what good you can do *right now* in this present moment. Instead of focusing on what makes you guilty, push yourself to focus on appreciating yourself. Focus on your virtues and accomplishments rather than the mistakes you've made or guilt you may feel.

Forget about the past and live in the present

You must create a firm grasp now on the present. The past is gone and it is not coming back. Ever. So what you need to do is let it go completely. It is safe to assume that you know you can't change the past, yes? Why is it that you cling to it then?

We have all done it at some point in time. I know I did. Have you ever wondered why you continue to hold on to and think about it constantly? It certainly doesn't benefit you to live in the past, because what has happened has happened. You must come to grips with this. No matter what happened, there is a solution.

Remember, live in the present. The present is all that is happening. Don't beat yourself up about the past ever again.

This step is *essential* to loving yourself and ultimately becoming well. Let go of bad memories. The only reason you can feel guilty about the past is if you continue remembering it. Let it go.

I can do it too!

Believe in yourself. Just because someone says something is hard, doesn't mean it has to be, and if it is, so what? Belief in yourself is the most important step to loving yourself. If you can believe in yourself, all things are possible for you.

If you see someone being successful in life, what makes you think you can't do the same? It's obviously doable right? If it were impossible to have success, nobody would be successful.

If something has been done, then it is possible. Create a mentality that says not only "I can," but "I will."

When you *will* something to happen, you have a plan and faith that it will happen. When you say, "I will beat my anxiety," you plan on it.

From now on, when you say, "I will," say it with a deep commitment, and believe that what you will is true for you.

Express yourself fully and honestly

This is so important. I can't stress enough how important this is. You must express your feelings and ideas. Anxiety is based on pent up feelings that haven't been expressed. I can attest to this because of the fact that I bottled up every single solitary feeling I had before I had my first full-blown panic attack. I never allowed myself to be me.

It was mainly because I worried excessively about how others would perceive me, and to such a degree that it deeply affected me later on, causing an anxiety related disorder. I kept all my feelings, problems, thoughts — just about everything — to myself. Does this sound like you? If so, you need to stop right now and think about how you are affected by not expressing yourself properly.

It may seem like an arbitrary step at first, but with time you will realize how important it is to allow yourself to *be yourself* at any given time. You will feel whole, complete, and have a deep connection and keen sense of the essence of who are. Allow yourself to be who you are, without wearing a mask or putting on a false front in the presence of others.

Remember that anxiety stems and grows from unconscious fears and beliefs you may have without realizing it. When someone puts on a false front they are not being themselves, and when someone isn't being him- or herself, it is because they fear what others think of them. They become so deeply concerned with the opinions of others that they repress themselves.

When you repress your emotions, they build inside of you. This kind of repression may have caused you to become anxious. However, that's not the issue. What matters now is what you will do about it. From now on, make it your objective to be you. Once you can fully and honestly express yourself, you will have already destroyed part of your anxiety. Remember, your anxiety disorder is simply a state of excessive worry, and a portion of the worry is due to your concern with other people's thoughts of you as you try and read their minds.

And once you can learn to feel good, you can shift your negative mindset to a positive one and begin your path to wellness.

S T4E P

YOUR PASSION

The next thing you need to do is discover your passion. This step will work great when properly utilized in alignment with expressing yourself and being assertive. This means that you should find something that really envelops your mind. Something that causes time to stop in your sense of awareness. Something that you could simply do forever and love every second of it. Something that diverts you from any problem no matter how big. Finding a passion is essential to becoming well, not to mention that it's much better to focus your time and energy on something you love to do rather than feeding your anxiety. It can be a hobby, a pastime, or anything that you enjoy doing.

Think about things that you love to do. Write them out on a sheet of paper. Here are some points to consider:

- What are you passionate about?
- What instills a deep and burning desire inside of you?
- What makes you feel good?
- What are you good at?
- What do you *want* to be good at?
- If you could make millions doing something that you love, what would that be?
- What is it that makes time just stop because of the fact that you love it so very much?
- What really makes you smile from ear to ear?
- What do you deeply enjoy?
- What could you dedicate your life to?
- What activity do you love every moment of?

As you brainstorm, keep in mind that some things require what I like to call *passive* and *active* thought. Things that require passive thought are based on your brain working through response, and don't require much concentration on your part, like watching T.V. for example.

Passive thought activities don't involve your behavior in any way; in fact, they barely involve your mind at all. When you are engaged in passive thought activities, you simply take something in and formulate a thought or a set of thoughts around it.

On the other hand, active thought activities involve your mind and body, and they work in tandem. When you are thinking actively, it means you are creating new thoughts in your mind, rather than *taking in* an image and using it as a base for thought.

Take painting for example. Painting a picture onto a canvas takes a lot of creativity. A person's mind is wholly used when painting a picture and the physical body is just as much a part of the creation as the artist's vision. The artist has to have steady hands, proper brush strokes, etc.

That's the key when finding a really deep passion, to find a passion that requires *active* thought. Remember, an activity requiring active thought involves you as a whole. It involves the mind *and* body.

Try to find something that takes creative rather than passive thought. This means doing something that requires you to have creative thoughts or to get up and move, such as writing, hiking, photography, painting, etc. Doing things that only require passive thought won't really divert you from your anxiety, but rather *remind* you of it because you are doing something which is comfortable and accommodating to your anxiety. This is not acceptable in your situation.

When you base something around your anxiety, you give it power. But when you do things that require active thoughts, you will distract yourself from your anxious thoughts, and shift your thinking to a more positive undertaking. You will use that entire powerful mind of yours towards something beneficial, rather than using it to perpetuate anxiety. Remember, your mind is absolutely brilliant. Once you take that brilliance and power of your mind and use it towards something useful, you will learn to experience joy and obliterate anxiety once and for all.

ACTION

A ction is the next order of business when getting rid of anxiety. This step is the most important step. It is critical and seriously needs to be implemented now. Otherwise, all that you've done to recover will have been for nothing, quite frankly. Hopefully by now, your attitude towards anxiety has changed, from negative to positive. What I mean by this is that you should now be clear that you are not mentally ill, that this is fixable, and that only you can do it. However, that new attitude alone will not get rid of it. Anxiety cannot simply be "thought" away on its own. All that effort you put towards transforming your way of thinking must now be offered in the name of precise and determined action.

I know it may be hard when you have anxiety, but you've got to get your butt off the couch and do something about it. Your anxiety isn't going to leave quietly. If you allow it to stay there, you better believe it will remain right there in your mind. You are the only one who can get you through this.

Your kids, coworkers, parents, or friends can definitely encourage you and push to keep you going, but in the end you are the only one who can change this. Think about it. These are *your* thoughts and *your* feelings. No one can understand them fully or control them other than you, because they are in *your* mind, and no one else's.

Anxiety keeps you from doing the things you would normally love to do. Things that are normally fun suddenly become a heavy burden, and that just sucks. Seriously, think about it. Why should you be afraid of things that you could be enjoying every day? I mean, come on! What kind of life revolves around fear?

As I stated before, this book is not here to help you cope or 'live with' anxiety, unless you'd call that living (I call it barely existing, if that).

You should *want* to take action. Get excited about it. Get animated. Get energized about finally being through with the nonsense that is anxiety and finally be able to go out and be a happy person again!

I really want you to become thrilled with the idea of being the 'normal you' again. Because once you're there, once you can finally breathe a true sigh of relief, once you can be comfortable with any and every situation that comes your way and seeing life with the most positive of attitudes, the taste of victory is ever so sweet. Not to mention the benefits that comes with such a success.

This is what I used to ask myself every single day... *Is this it? Am I going to live this way for the rest of my life?* Then, I would immediately tell myself, *No. This is not what my life was meant to be. I'm better than this.* I would constantly focus on where I wanted to be — a healthy, happy, and non-anxious person.

I'd like you to do the same; to ask yourself this very same question. *Do I really want to live this way for the rest of my life? If I had the ability change this right now, would I do it, no matter what it takes?*

Please appreciate the fact that you need to believe that you deserve to be well. You certainly don't deserve to live anxiously, that's for sure. No one does. Bear in mind again that the purpose of this book is not to teach you how to exist with anxiety or learn coping techniques. This book calls and challenges you to take action, that action being the steps and procedures aimed at the health and wellness of your mind. This is absolutely, positively the most important step in this book.

Now that you have shifted your approach to your anxiety, you need to kick it into high gear.

Remember that little part of your brain we talked about earlier, the Amygdala? Well, it only responds to *behavior*. You won't be able to just think the change into existence.

The only reason your anxiety continues to perpetuate as it does is because of the fact that you have not only been thinking anxiously, but also *behaving* anxiously. That's the key. Behavior.

The Amygdala only responds to how you go about your life. It takes the way you act on a regular basis (the way you walk, talk, etc.) and formulates habits for you based upon those actions. Naturally, this is meant to help you, because who would want to think consciously about how to behave all the time?

Habits allow us to do things without thinking about them, allowing us to focus on other things simultaneously. However, there are bad habits that can be created after performing a negative behavior repeatedly. As stated before, your anxiety is essentially a bad habit. It is a habituated and negative way of thinking, feeling, and acting, and it is negative simply because of the fact that it does not feel good and serves no positive purpose.

The only way to be truly rid of anxiety and its remnants is to change the way you act. This step is going to take quite a bit of effort on your part. It's a very simple part of the program, but it is absolutely the most important step, because this part of the procedure is where changes happen.

You must understand that it is absolutely imperative that you follow this step along with the others as these steps only work when they move together in proper alignment. Do them all, and do them correctly.

The first order of business is to begin to withdraw medications if you are already taking them. Of course you'll want to do this under the supervision of your doctor.

In my case I never began taking any kind of medication. I refused to begin taking drugs, and this was a wise decision for me, because in my opinion these medications never really help with the underlying causes of anxiety.

No medication rids anyone of the anxiety, it just alleviates the symptoms. In other words, prescription drugs like diazepam may appear to fix your anxiety but in reality the medication just staves it off until your next dose. The root cause of the anxiety is still there, even though it feels good for the moment to believe otherwise.

Sometimes the anxious feelings come back stronger causing some to become dependent on these medications. Talk to your doctor about setting up some kind of withdrawal program for you.

Based upon my own experience, the only way for you to be truly one hundred percent anxiety free is to make changes in your thinking, behavior, and your overall lifestyle. The best way to do this is to *expose* yourself to what makes you feel anxious. This is absolutely crucial to be well once again. Think about what it is that makes you feel anxious. Now, imagine being able to be exposed to whatever triggers your anxiety, and feeling as relaxed as you are right now while reading this book. Wouldn't that be nice? Does it sound impossible? Well, it isn't. The result of your actions as you learn to change your behavior is that you will able to face and confront whatever makes you anxious, and you will be able to do it all on your own.

So let's say that you are afraid of being around people, as this is quite common. Start by recognizing your feelings and the sensations that accompany them. Don't fight those sensations because they will receive more credibility and power if you do.

Instead, just feel them. Think to yourself, *these are just people. I'm a person too. There's nothing to be afraid of.* Indeed this is true, for the people you are around are simply human beings like you. They're no different, and you're no different.

Go to the mall, a party, or enjoy a night out with friends. Start out small if you have to. Go to the grocery store and buy a gallon of milk and don't be afraid to be friendly and make eye contact with the cashier (don't forget to smile!). As you allow yourself less time to dwell on anxiety, you will begin to feel more comfortable. Learn to challenge yourself constantly, no matter how uncomfortable you may feel at first. Get used to being around people, and be excited about it! Humans are naturally wired to like being around others. There's truly no reason to fear one another.

S T 6 E P

DETACH

There are a few concepts I learned from studying Zen that helped me get over my own anxiety. I approached it by looking at it as a philosophy and as a way of thinking and living peacefully. One concept of Zen that I found really helpful with anxiety and fear in general is the concept of *detachment* or *detached mind.*

Detachment / Detached Mind

The concept of detachment or detached mind is an extremely simple concept, which is why it is so brilliant.

Detachment gives a person true freedom from what people would normally consider burdensome. The ability to detach yourself from and to let go of negativity is true freedom in every sense. Think about that.

If you could experience anything, and feel either neutral or great, wouldn't that make life so much more pleasant, not to mention a lot easier? With detachment, nothing can ever get you down in the dumps anymore. Nothing will make you sad or depressed, and besides, why must that ever happen in the first place?

Ask yourself this: *Why should something outside of myself control how I think and feel?* Indeed, why should anything influence how you feel (I say "influence" because after all, in the end you are the master in control of your thoughts, feelings, and actions, whether you realize it or not, whether you believe it or not)?

The primary principle behind detachment is to be able to experience any kind of situation without becoming overly affected by it. Detachment allows you to be able to let go of any sort of negativity. So any time in your life that you encounter something less than wonderful, such as getting a traffic ticket for example, you can let it go with a detached mind.

The concept is simple, but may take a bit of mental rewiring on your part since you may not be used to it. Let's use receiving a traffic ticket as the example. All that you have to do is realize that what has happened, has happened. Nothing will change the fact that you just received a ticket. Therefore, there is no reason to dwell on that big evil policeman who wrote you a citation for speeding.

Your job is to just let it go. The purpose of using detachment is to be able to have experiences throughout your life without becoming too attached to those experiences, whether they are negative or positive.

The idea is that you take what you are experiencing currently and accept it. By "accept it," I don't mean to imply that you should simply roll over, play dead, and take anything that comes your way. The idea is that you let go of your current circumstance, look at it with either a positive or neutral perspective, and then move on.

If something positive happens, great. Enjoy it as much as you can for as long as it lasts. If something negative happens to you, keep a neutral mental and emotional position. Instead of saying, "Oh foo! Woe is me!" learn to say, "Well, that's what is." and move forward. That's the key when using the concept of detachment.

When you move forward, you forgive, forget, and allow yourself to grow. It makes more sense to continue on after all, doesn't it? I'm assuming we can agree that nothing can change the past right? Granted, I'm not saying that you should become a stone cold, emotionally bereft person who instantly forgets something like the death of a loved one.

What I am saying, however, is that you shouldn't cling to sad memories; rather, learn to let go of them after some time. So in the event that you do experience bereavement, accept that the person has passed on. Feel the grief. Feel the sadness. Don't fight the feelings. Then, let them go.

As you learn to let go in a more proficient manner, you may eventually learn to free yourself of feelings such as guilt or depression completely. You may even end up being able to look at any experience that someone else would consider negative with a detached perspective, getting rid of anxiety in the process.

Anxiety thrives on guilt, because with guilt you affirm to yourself that there is something wrong with you, that you are inferior in some way. Guilt is the central hub of anxiety, second only to the feeling of fear itself.

I really took this idea of the detached mind to heart. I began to simply live in the moment. I figured that if depersonalization was here to stay, I would make the best of it, since being afraid of it wouldn't really do anything but make me feel worse.

I started to examine how I could *utilize* depersonalization to my advantage, how I could get it to serve me, instead of pondering day in and day out about how I could figure out a way to get rid of it. *Huh?* Exactly.

I let go of the attachment to the idea that I had to get rid of anxiety and depersonalization, because I was looking at depersonalization with a detached mind. So how did I use this seemingly horrible state of mind to my benefit? Depersonalization was both a blessing and a curse. Sure, I couldn't tell if anything was real, and that scared me. However, that was all that scared me, and nothing else did, because the world around me didn't feel real.

So in losing the ability to feel what reality was, nothing could scare me, because I made no attachment or connection to it.

I recognized this consciously, and decided to use it to my advantage. I would dive into any and every situation that would make me feel uncomfortable at first, but soon I was able to let go of that discomfort because I focused on how unreal it was to me. To begin using the concept of detached mind, you are going to reprogram your mind a bit, mainly because of the fact this is not something you learned in school, and your parents probably didn't raise you with it either. Therefore, this is going to take a bit of work on your part as you begin to look at life with a completely transformed perspective.

Another thing I realized is that people become so attached to negative events in their lives, and pay little or no heed to the positive ones. You have probably been able to focus really hard on what has gone wrong in your life, whether due to anxiety or other things. My challenge to you is this: Take all of that energy that you put into concentrating on negativity and pain, and put it towards what is good in your life instead. You will begin to feel better immediately.

This is an activity that requires active thought, because you must consciously focus on the good things in life that you are grateful for, and hopefully take the action to recognize it.

Halt Repression

Repression is when a person suppresses their true needs, problems, and even personality traits within themselves. Repression is a huge no-no. Repression sets the stage for anxiety, because it is a belief system that revolves around worrying what others think. And with worry, comes anxiety.

You may be repressing yourself without even realizing it, and I admit that I had a serious problem with repressing myself, and I have no excuses (affirming once again that anxiety is caused by the sufferer). This is where depersonalization helped me.

I used depersonalization to sever any connection that I had to any worries of what others thought of me, because that's all they were, thoughts. Then came the realization: *Thoughts can't hurt me. So who cares?* It makes sense doesn't it? When you repress yourself, you fear someone's thoughts.

First of all, you don't really know what a person thinks about you. So why should you try and be a mind reader? Forget about what a person *might* be thinking about you, and focus on how they treat you instead.

What is fear, and how do we conquer it?

I mentioned fear several times in previous chapters throughout this book, and how your fears ultimately cause anxiety.

Have you ever taken the time to ask yourself, *what is fear?* Have you ever asked yourself why fear exists, or why you feel it on such a consistent basis? If you could sit down and describe what it is to feel fear, what would you say? How would you describe what you feel during those frightening moments?

Would you portray the thoughts that play in your mind or the physical sensations that you may experience? Would you say it's that pounding in your chest, that skyrocketing heart rate?

Or maybe you would describe it as butterflies in your stomach. What about that tension in your muscles or the cold sweat you get when you're really on the edge?

Fear has allowed numerous species on the planet to survive for eons; those fight or flight responses that have allowed the various organisms on our planet to continue thriving for all of these years. Fear is normally triggered by a dangerous object or situation, ranging from dealing with predators in the wild or walking down a dark alley in The Bronx.

When a person or animal feels fear, they quite naturally associate that feeling with danger. They also remember what caused them to feel scared, so the next time they come across that object or situation, they will remember the fear they felt before. As they feel threatened, they will either deal with that object or situation in some way, by fighting and/or avoiding it.

Fear is a defense mechanism in normal cases. It is a healthy thing to be afraid when faced with a potential hazard. However, in the case of someone with an anxiety or panic disorder, a person may become fearful of things that aren't actually dangerous at all. Whether or not the object or situation is dangerous, a person will avoid it when the fear becomes too unpleasant.

In most cases, fear is nothing more than seeing yourself somewhere in the future in a highly undesirable or unpleasant situation. For example, if you are afraid of sharks, you are seeing yourself in the future, being attacked or even eaten by a shark. Very undesirable and unpleasant indeed!

Here is a very simple way to breakdown any fear you may have. It works with all fear, because every fear in a person's mind is composed of three base elements:

- The stimulus
- The change or result that could be brought by that stimulus
- The uncomfortable feelings and sensations brought on by the thought of that change

The **stimulus** is the object or situation that *stimulates* you to think and behave in a certain way. It is what you perceive outside of yourself which you process in your mind, thereby causing you to feel a certain way.

This could be something positive, such as receiving a present from someone you love, which makes you smile and feel good. Obviously in the case of fear, it could also be something negative that naturally causes you to become worried for your own safety.

However, as you already know, this isn't exactly what you are afraid of. If you think that this is what causes you to feel scared, think again, and read on.

The stimulus that you encounter causes you to predict the **change or result** brought on by it. Your mind begins to try and piece together what will happen after encountering that object. For example, if you are afraid of physically fighting (the stimulus), the result you think of is of your body being broken in some way or even being killed.

The change almost always involves one or both of these things: Physical harm and/or being in other types of trouble or dilemma.

In terms of being afraid of physical harm, this is totally natural and is beneficial to the survival of a species. People and animals fundamentally exist because of how they have learned to avoid situations that can cause them harm. It's all in the name of survival.

When you can break down your fears in this manner, you will ultimately overcome them. As you have noticed, it's all about your feelings towards the object. The fear of something always comes down to what you *feel*. Once you can control how you feel, rather than letting how you're feeling control you, you will infallibly conquer any and every fear you have, and eventually lead a much happier life.

And what are the main sources of unhappiness?

Fear.

People are afraid of things like change, whether the change is negative or positive. When someone is in their comfort zone, they figure *hey, it's nice here. Why leave now when I'm nice and cozy?*

People are afraid of leaving their comfort zone, simply because they don't want to or are afraid to experience discomfort. Then, they wonder why their life is so mundane and boring.

I now challenge you to leave your comfort zone. Attack any fear that you may have. Let yourself get comfortable with these feelings, and really push them. Remember, don't fight them, but allow your fears to get as seemingly bad as they may, and watch as you begin to have a much tighter grip on your own mind and so much more control over your emotions.

It's a very empowering thing once you've mastered control of your own mind, and it really can't be that hard if you think about it. It's *your* mind. Therefore it would seem logical that you should be able to control it. The truth is that you can, and it's easier than you think.

Fear is a state of being where one is emotionally and mentally unprepared for something. For example, if someone fears mice, they are unprepared to deal with the emotional and mental disturbances associated with encountering mice.

They may say things like, "Mice are disgusting! Just look at their tails and how nasty they look!" In their mind, mice cause them to feel uncomfortable, and they associate the mouse's tail and anything else they don't like about mice with those discomforting feelings.

Then, when they try to explain those feelings of discomfort and fear, it comes out as, "Mice are disgusting," or, "they're so gross," rather than, "I feel very uncomfortable when I see a mouse." Most of the time people don't understand why they are afraid of mice. After all, a mouse is just an animal like any other, right? Think about it. It has legs, ears, eyes, etc. Yet for some reason someone may feel differently about a mouse than they would a cat or a dog. Have you ever asked yourself why that is? It's because when a person says that they have a fear of mice, they are actually unable to handle the unpleasant feelings and thoughts that come about when they encounter a mouse.

As for fear in general, it's all the same. It is because they have associated that certain thing, place, or person with those familiar dreadful feelings.

The key to conquering any and every fear that you have is to learn to get and continue to be *comfortable* with those normally distressing feelings or thoughts.

Don't be afraid to feel the fear within you. Let it flow through you, and simply let it go.

Never mind the thing that's causing you to feel the fear inside of you. Let that go, and focus instead on the feeling itself. If you can convince yourself that the only thing causing you to feel afraid of something is you, then you will transcend every fear that you have.

Be warned however. Fear is there to protect you from danger. If you have a fear of lions and decide to conquer it and go wrestling a lion in Africa, you may very well get yourself killed. Sometimes we do need fear, and sometimes we don't. Wrestling lions falls under 'do'.

Any fear can be conquered in 3 easy steps:

Acknowledge the stimulus and any result you associate with encountering it, the feelings of fear, and only regard them as natural sensations.

Relax into the sensations associated with feeling fear, letting them flow through your body and mind without affecting you.

Then . . .

Let the feelings go.

This formula is the best method to transcend any and every fear imaginable. It is so mind twistingly simple yet so powerful. The key to the first step is to not try and run away from your fears. What you must do is allow yourself to look at your fear. Allow yourself to encounter that stimulus. Admit to yourself what you feel. Recognize the feelings of fear, and don't be afraid to *feel them*. Allow yourself to give in to those uncomfortable sensations within you. Don't fight them.

Realize that the feeling is the same no matter what causes it, whether it is caused by heights, spiders, lions, numbers, people, etc.

Once you can convince yourself to be comfortable with those feelings and sensations, you will instantly be comfortable with whatever causes it, because remember: it's not the object that you are afraid of, it's the feeling.

When you get used to the sensations, you become comfortable with the stimulus that you feel fearful towards, thus you conquer whatever fear that you may have. I use this technique on a daily basis. That's really all it takes. These steps are so incredibly simple and easy.

Still, I'd be disingenuous if I said that you would skate through this with ease. The main thing that will affect the speed of your progress is the level of control you have over your mind, because as you begin to go against your routine thought patterns, it will seem like you are lying to yourself at first.

Your mind will try and tell you that you're wrong over and over. It will tell you that those irrational fears are real and that you must avoid those friendly people or that workplace environment.

What you must do is use that logical power that your mind has to see the truth of what is and is not a danger to your well being.

Don't allow your current unconscious perception of what is dangerous to keep you from experiencing life. Learn to believe that those irrational fears that you have are indeed irrational. Get comfortable with feeling those unpleasant sensations within you and then convince yourself of what is truly dangerous and what isn't.

The purpose of all of this is to one day totally release the idea of fear itself. Ideally, you will be able to quickly cast away fear as though it is an illusion, a hallucination.

Look at fear as something that isn't real. Look at it as something that doesn't exist in any way shape, fashion, or form. Dismiss the very concept of fear.

This is going to take a bit of getting used to, but it is quite easy and simple. Naturally, this is a perfect concept to put into practice whether you suffer from anxiety or would just like to learn to control fear.

Some may say, "But the fear is real! I can feel it!" To those people, I propose this next simple example. Take dreams for instance. You know that what you just saw wasn't real when you wake up in the morning. That zombie that ate your brains last night was never really there. However, for the time that it was playing in your head, it was very real, and you felt how real the experience was.

The reason for this is that the subconscious mind doesn't know the difference between what is real or not.

That's where your conscious mind comes in. It allows you to discern between reality and delusion, and you consciously decide that for yourself.

If you can consciously decide that fear isn't real for you and then make it a habit, you can bet your life that you will beat anxiety and ultimately any fear in general. Moreover, if you can apply it while you are feeling the unpleasant and anxious sensations as you go about confronting your fear, you will quickly become desensitized to it, and it will go away soon after, if not instantly.

Think of confronting your anxiety as trying something new or exciting. As you feel the anxious feelings, remember that they are just feelings, little tingles. Let them simply flow, and even ask for more. Remember, all of the various sensations you experience all revolve around and come down to one thing. *Fear.* As you build the habit of taking your fears and systematically conquering them one by one, you will quickly run out of things to be scared or anxious about.

This may be the hardest step for you as an anxiety sufferer, because it requires action, and that action may cause you to become frightened since you have to do it on your own. Remember that no one is feeling what you are feeling besides you. You must come to terms with this. You have to do this alone.

However, don't be afraid to tell family and friends what you're going through, as they may not totally understand.

Don't make the same mistake I made by not telling anyone. There are people who care about you, and it isn't fair that you shut yourself away from them as they worry about you and wonder what is wrong. Just let them know what you're dealing with, and be brief about it. There's no need to go into detail, because you'll give the anxiety power if you do.

Just tell them that you have anxiety, and that you are going through hell, but don't get too deep. Just keep them informed. Give them an idea of what is going on with you. Allowing people to know what you are presently going through is important because it makes it a lot easier if you have support, after all. So, next time someone asks, "What's wrong," you should simply say something to the effect of, "I have some anxiety problems that I'm going through right now, but not for much longer."

If they ask you to elaborate, go ahead and maybe tell them what worries you, but don't get carried away and talk about it for hours on end because you will just go back to where you started. This holds true when people ask you about anxiety in the future after you have risen above it.

If someone asks you about your previous bouts with anxiety, tell them, "Yeah, I was anxious," and leave it at that.

It may not seem like it now, but what you are currently going through with your anxiety is a great time. As you have continued to live with these feelings of fear and anxiety day after day, it's safe to say they've become commonplace, right? Because of this you will have an edge that no one else has once you come out of anxiety. This is because the majority of people don't experience fear and anxiety for such long periods of time as an anxiety-ridden person does.

If I experience any kind of situation that would normally make someone scared, I would simply think, *Been there, done that,* because fear always feels the same way, every time. I simply allow myself to get used to those feelings of fear and anxiety after having dealt with them for so long, and you will do the same.

After dealing with anxiety, you will realize just as I did that there is really no reason to be afraid of anything at all, especially those silly and irrational fears.

Act fast, and act true. Try to do everything you can with commitment, dedication, and efficiency. In your effort to get rid of fear or anxiety remember that we are creatures of habit, so create positive habits of doing everything to the best of your ability. As you do this, your unconscious mind will continue to get you into the habit of doing things in the best, most effective and efficient way possible. The habit of excellence.

When you act in this pleasant manner with no thoughts given over to fear or anxiety, you will quickly be well.

S T 7 E P

SELF MASTERY

I want to congratulate you on making it this far. This is a great turning point in your life. After you emerge from this condition, you will be wiser and mentally stronger. You will be wiser because of all of the new things you will learn about yourself while going through this process. You will be stronger because you have learned how to be in control of your own mind, and how you handle any fear that you may feel. Hopefully by now you have been able to put the previous steps into practice. Maybe you have even begun to relax, understand what you are feeling, love and appreciate yourself more, find a passion, and have started to take decisive and unwavering action.

Now it's time to implement the final step: Self Mastery.

The concept of self-mastery allows you to do exactly what it implies. You must now become the master of yourself, and realize the true level of control that one should always maintain. As the master of yourself, you shall be able to face life as you always should, with your chin high and paying no heed to negativity.

Self-mastery will set up a strong and sturdy foundation in you. This base will create a drive within that will be there for you, pushing you to make the best of yourself every day rather than acting in response to whatever your fears tell you.

There are three steps to mastering yourself:

Release — The ability to release anxiety through releasing negativity (guilt, anger, fear, etc.) and creating the healthy habit of *feeling good*.

Control — The ability to remain in control in any given situation.

Live — Learn to have a zest for life and simply "play the game."

These elements work in tandem with one another and they all essentially mean the same thing. When you have one, you will have the other. When you release negativity, you are in control. When you are dismissing things like anger, fear, and anxiety, you will allow yourself to keep control in any situation. As you will soon find out, control starts with you. And when you can have control over yourself — over your mind — you will ultimately be in control, whatever the circumstance.

When you release negativity by allowing it to flow through your mind without it affecting you, or simply paying no heed to it, then you are truly in control

When you can allow yourself to live your life with a certain zest and without the burdens of negativity, you will find that you become a happier, more contented person. Let's look at each of these steps a little more in-depth.

Release

Now you must learn how to allow yourself to **release** your anxiety and liberate yourself, once and for all. This step is simple because it doesn't take much on your part. This step is also crucial to the whole puzzle, because this step involves *allowing* yourself to forget about anxiety. You are the only one who can let it go. It all begins with releasing any negativity that you may have within yourself. Pay zero attention to pessimism, disapproval, etc.

It may seem like a complicated task, but it really isn't. The concept is truly easy to implement. You now know that you have learned, habituated, and perpetuated anxious thought and behavior because of all the attention, credibility, and merit that you give it.

All it takes is a change in your awareness. Just as you've done with anxious thoughts and behaviors, all you have to do now is learn, habituate, and perpetuate *non*-anxious thoughts and behaviors. Essentially, you are simply redirecting what you did previously, focusing instead on non-anxious rather than anxious behavior.

A good way to start is by learning to do things for the sake of enjoyment. You need to start doing things because you simply *want* to do them. In other words, don't do something in an attempt to eliminate your anxiety.

I know that it may seem like I'm tossing another paradox at you, but I assure you that I'm not. What I'm saying is that you must learn how to enjoy the things that you are doing as you endeavor to do away with anxiety without thinking about them as just a form of therapy.

You have probably been carrying out the previous steps in this book as a method of *fighting* anxiety (remember, fighting anxiety only makes it stronger). For example, say in an effort to combat your anxiety, you went out with friends in order to divert yourself from or even to combat the sensations associated with anxiety.

This isn't wrong because it got the ball rolling. And after taking action, you proved to yourself that you are capable of winning. However, as you continue *fighting* against your anxiety, you continue to insist that it still exists in some way within you.

Now is the time to change all of that. What you must do now is enjoy your pursuits for the sole purpose of enjoyment. Go out with your friends for the sole reason of wanting to have a good time. Enjoy the day with people that you care about and have the fun you've been missing for so long.

Go workout only for the sake of improving your physical health. Focus your attention on overcoming that weight or running for that extra ten minutes. Do you see the difference?

On the one hand you were acting on your anxiety. You were doing some activity because you were thinking about trying to fight and rid yourself of the anxiety. On the other hand, you are simply doing those things for the sake of your own satisfaction and enjoyment. Do something that you enjoy, just for the sake of enjoying it and feeling good, without any thought of anxiety.

You need to learn to **feel good** on a consistent basis. Feelings are truly what make people tick. The ultimate need that every human being on earth seeks is to feel good. No matter what goals someone may set in their lifetime, it is always the feeling of attaining them that is paramount. It's the feelings that arrive when achieving a particular goal that makes it all worthwhile.

Anything and everything that we do in life always comes down to what we feel, every time, no exception. And how you feel is truly up to you. You are ultimately in control of how you feel. Nothing can change the way you feel — for better or worse — unless you give it permission.

And when it comes to the negative aspects of life, learn to simply refer to these as experiences, and let go of the negativity that you associate them. Learn to embrace the positive more often, and in doing so, you will begin to feel better.

People often go through life paying no heed to their need for happiness and love because they have bills to be paid, mouths to feed, and taxes to file.

They get so heavily bent up and focused on their duties that they lose sight of themselves and their own needs, and as a result they tend to progressively feel worse. At the same time, these same people get so self-obsessed to the point that they can only focus on how bad they feel, rather than how they can learn to feel good.

For some reason it has become commonplace that feeling overworked and tired is acceptable, that almost every hard-working person must feel bad. In addition people everywhere pay more attention to the crappiness they *do* feel rather than the goodness they *can and should feel.* Feeling bad all the time is more acceptable than feeling good all the time.

But if people knew the how their mind affects them, they would surely change their ways. Your mind has a huge impact on your health and well-being. Too much stress can actually make you sick! So if you think that feelings mean nothing, do yourself a favor and think again.

Don't think for a second that going after good feelings is a trivial pursuit. The emotional needs of people are just as important, just as necessary, and just as vital to a person's health as food, water, shelter, and sleep.

Feelings are what make you and me human. Just as you fill your stomach with food when you are hungry, you need to fulfill your emotional needs, too. I used to be a person who paid literally zero attention to fulfilling my emotional needs. I wouldn't allow myself to express my emotions in any way. I knew that I hated every second of it, but for some silly reason I thought it was wrong to allow myself to be human, and express those emotions.

Silly me.

I wanted to somehow be perfect, and throughout my life I tried to achieve that impossible goal. It got to the point where I behaved "like a machine" as my dad once said, and I knew he was right. During this time I was a real loner, and regarded the gift of the ability to feel as wrong. Can you believe that? I used to think that it was wrong to have feelings! What a bunch of bunk!

Obviously I was being completely silly and absurd, but for some reason, that's what I thought was true. This was before I knew about depersonalization, and looking back on it now, I definitely had an anxiety problem at the time. But I didn't know it.

I really thought I had it all figured out at the age of fifteen. Boy was I mistaken. On a more positive note, I can now say that I truly feel good every day of my life.

I express myself fully and honestly in every way, and so must you. You deserve it.

Sure, I may have my share of troubles every now and then, but they don't affect me like they used to. After going through anxiety and truly having a good hard look at myself and my mind, I have changed my perceptions of life to reflect a more positive point of view, and now you can too, because the steps outlined in this book are the exact ones that I took myself.

A great way I have found to feel terrific is to wake up with a positive and grateful attitude. Having a positive and grateful attitude will encourage you to feel good for the rest of the day. You would be amazed at how much your entire day changes just because of how you started it.

If you do this every morning you won't need that extra cup of coffee or the energy drink because you will draw the energy to get you going through yourself. Imagine that.

Wouldn't it be nice to spring out of bed in the morning with joy for what lies ahead? It's a lot easier than you may think.

Wake up with love in your heart. Before, I would wake up feeling ridiculously exhausted, even if I got seven or more hours of sleep. I would think *I've gotta get up now,* and I'd proceed to reluctantly drag myself out of bed with dread and toss myself into the shower.

Now when I wake up each morning, I say, "Praise God that I have another day. Life is good. I'm still breathing, and I'm going to make it a point to feel good today," no matter how tired or crappy I may feel getting up. It is a simple exercise you can do every day. When you get up in the morning and say, "I'm going to make it a point to feel good today," or simply "Thank you." Say it with intention, and truly mean and believe it from the bottom of your heart.

Say it with love and keen awareness. Believe that wonderful things will happen to you today. Expect that today is a good day. Make it your goal to feel good right when you wake up, because when you do you start the day on such a higher level of being then you would if you moaned and groaned about how bad you feel.

By continuously feeling good, you will naturally forget about anxiety. You will be able to enjoy life in all its splendor with a renewed vigor, vitality, energy, and drive.

Control

Everybody wants to have control, whether it is control of their finances, health, relationships, or just their lives in general. However, people tend to seek this control by trying to control others. People try to tell each other what to do in order to hopefully fulfill what they want to see happen for themselves.

Some think that if they can get others to do what they want at anytime, then that is control. However, this is not the type of control you need to establish for yourself.

For some odd reason, we always point at others for our problems. It always has to be somebody else's fault. Control begins with you taking responsibility for your own life. Let go of the attachment to who you think has wronged you in some way. Let all of that go and begin to look inward.

Look to yourself.

Most people overlook the fact that they can be in control of any situation if they simply learn to control themselves. When you can be in control of your thoughts, emotions, and actions in any situation imaginable, you will always be in control.

Having control of yourself will allow you to handle a situation in the most efficient way possible. When you can be in control of yourself, your thoughts will remain clear, collected, and concise. Imagine being at the beach on a most beautiful, sunny day. The sky is incredibly blue, and there's not a cloud to be seen. What's going through your mind at a time like this? How do you feel? How do you behave?

You probably feel relaxed, safe, and in control, because you can come and go as you please. Now imagine being able to feel that same way when faced with a dangerous or otherwise undesirable situation. If you can be relaxed and calm to such a degree in a dangerous situation that you can continue to operate at ease, then you can bet your life that you are most certainly in control.

The level of control that you have over yourself will ultimately determine the outcome. The level of control will dictate how you think and make decisions for yourself, whether in a dangerous situation or in some other scenario. As you are able to be in command of your mind, you will handle life's obstacles with the utmost of ease, because even if something gets in your way, it won't affect you.

You will look at your circumstances through a neutral and detached perspective, and in doing so you will act with efficiency to overcome your obstacle, rather than grieve over how hard it is for you.

Think about it. Would it be easier for a group of businessmen to handle a negotiation by screaming at one another for hours? Or should they all sit down at a table and discuss their proposals with clear, collect, and concise minds?

The absolute best way to be in control is to simply let go of the need for control. *What?* Yes. The way to be in control is to release yourself of your attachment of wanting to be in control. The only reason one would fear loss of control is due to their attachment to pursuing or struggling to keep control.

Dismiss the desperation for control. What you need to do is focus on taking full possession of your own mind and keep it at peace. Learn to adapt to your present circumstance instead of fighting what goes on around you. The ability to practice adaptation comes when you let go of the need to control anything outside of yourself. Once you can control yourself and your own mind, you will experience true freedom.

The idea that you might want to grasp here is that control begins with yourself. Only when you can control your own thoughts, feelings, and actions will you be able to truly control the various aspects of your life. It all begins with you. It begins with your thoughts, followed by your feelings, followed by your actions.

Remember, it all comes down to how you feel, each and every time, because your feelings will ultimately dictate how you act. If you keep yourself in a positive state of mind, you are in control. If you fall into a negative state of mind, you will feel that you have no control. One feels that they have no control only because they feel that something else outside of themselves has control over them. Your thoughts will affirm this lack of control based on how you react to what you see around you, and you will act in accordance with those feelings resulting from those thoughts, perpetuating your lack of that control which you seek.

On the other (more positive) hand, your positive thoughts and feelings will shape a better perspective for you, and your actions will follow those thoughts and feelings for the betterment of your life. You will then form clear and concise plans for that betterment.

A clear plan is only possible through your own feeling of control. When you are taking charge of your mind, you are in control. You can begin to take control once you are able to realize that you are truly the master of your own destiny. It's as simple as that. Allow yourself to be unafraid; to take full responsibility for your own life. You have learned that you are the one who causes your anxiety, and you are equally capable of ending it. You can live anxiety-free, and with control you have the power to make it so.

I really got a chance to practice control of myself when I got into a car accident. Naturally, I was worried about the other party and how my life would change as a result of this.

Gazing at the airbags dangling out of my steering wheel and passenger side dashboard, I knew that my car was totaled, and I knew that it was the end of my clean driving record. However, I told myself that none of that mattered now. What happened, happened, and nothing was going to magically change it. I let this sink in right away, and I focused on how to handle the moment in the most efficient manner.

I shut my mind to any panic, and I got out of my car to check on the other party and make sure that everyone was okay. Shortly after the other party dialed 911, a traffic safety officer, an ambulance, and the fire department arrived. The ambulance and fire department left shortly after since our cars weren't in flames and no one was injured. To keep a long story short, all went smoothly. I shook hands with the driver, and we went our separate ways, agreeing that stuff like this just happens sometimes.

Once the whole ordeal was over, I truly felt that everything was going to be all right, and I held the deep faith that I would be able to handle any events resulting from the car accident.

Read that last sentence again. The moment you are able to have faith in yourself—that you will be able to handle whatever consequences may come your way—is the moment that you transcend fear.

In believing that all would be well, I let go of any fear, because remember when we feel scared, we're just trying to tell the future. We try to make sense of the current situation by imagining ourselves in a future situation that causes us discomfort, and then become afraid of that discomfort in the present.

I simply felt the discomfort, let it go, and moved on to handle the state of affairs in a competent and efficient manner. I was actually surprised at how I handled the circumstances and myself in general. Let the unknown be unknown. That's the key. If you are unsure about what will happen, let it be. You aren't supposed to be able to know the future. That's what makes life interesting.

Don't worry about what bad things the future *might* hold. Focus on the present, and act in a manner that is responsible for the future. Let your life unfold in front of you and spend your life in every moment you have.

Everything that has happened in your life is an **effect** that can be traced back to a **cause**. Take your anxiety disorder for instance.

The anxiety disorder you live with is the effect. If you really want to get rid of anxiety once and for all, all you have to do is eliminate the cause. The causes of your anxiety problem are your anxious thoughts and feelings, which then lead to the effect of your anxious actions.

All you have to do now is use the steps explained in this book to eliminate those causes, anxious thoughts and feelings. If you replace them with thoughts and feelings of relief and wellness your actions will follow suit. Once you fully realize that you are responsible for your own destiny, that *you* are the captain of your ship, nothing has to be hard anymore. All you have to do now is embrace your life, and live it.

Live

Life is simply way too short to waste it on anxiety. There is so much more to living than having to worry about how you will get through the day, or about what will go wrong, or any other foolish thoughts. You know that this is true. You know inside of you that you are meant to be well and free of this nonsense. Therefore, there is no reason at all for you to continue to allow an anxiety disorder to rule your life.

If you feel inspired to take action, take action. Don't sit by and wait for something to happen. When you feel ready to practice letting go of your fears, don't simply sit there and do nothing. Act with faith and diligence.

If you feel that you are ready to confront the object(s) of your fear, don't wait for it to show up. Go find it. Show yourself to it. Go confront your fear with a conviction and deeply burning belief in yourself that you will win. It all gets easier and easier when you begin to take faithful and responsible action. There's only light at the end of the tunnel.

It's all up to you now. The tools to be rid of anxiety forever have been presented to you in this book. Each and every step that has been described to you is exactly what you need to be free of any sort of fear — forever. With these steps it is yours to conquer any and every fear that you may have. Trust and expect that you will be well, because only you can order yourself to rise above this affliction that is stealing your quality of life.

Live with *you* in mind, and leave anxiety behind. Enjoy the ride, because life doesn't have to be a chore. The very act of being alive is a true blessing in itself. If you could only have one thing to be grateful for, that's all you need right there. Living.

Allow yourself to live each day with a healthily positive perspective, always moving forward no matter what. I learned to look at my anxiety a bit differently after I realized that I was literally afraid of nothing. I stopped calling it anxiety, and simply said to myself, "I'm just being silly. There's absolutely nothing to be afraid of." That's it.

I simply regarded my anxiety disorder as fleeting, short-lived silliness. I stopped naming every little symptom I felt. I stopped lamenting over whether this ordeal would be over, whether I would get better or not. I stopped looking for answers to what I was feeling because I realized that there was no solution to my anxiety disorder other than myself.

Allow yourself to play the game of life and not to get yourself too attached to any negative experiences that you may encounter along the way. If something negative happens, so what? No big deal. Let it go and move on.

Life is simply way too short to waste it on anxiety, negativity, or anything else that would interfere with happiness. Just get up in the morning and live without becoming stuck on mistakes and the guilt of the past. Move on. Do your best every single moment of your life. Spend your moments wisely.

Focus on today. Focus on now.

As you continue to practice the seven simple steps to transcend anxiety, you will conquer any and every fear that you have. You will live knowing your purpose. You will live with strength in your heart. You will live with your positive outlook and excitement for what tomorrow holds. You will live with a zest and passion for life itself.

You will live with nothing to fear.

ABOUT THE AUTHOR

Hady Elmashhady is a person driven by the passions in his life including the martial arts, earning a belt rank every year until he was 17. Following the last belt rank he earned, Hady immersed himself in the martial art of Muay Thai which he excels at and enjoys immensely. He applies the lessons he has learned in the dojo and the gym to various aspects of his life. Hady and his family are originally of Egyptian heritage. He was born in Manama, Bahrain. His family moved to the United States in 1994 where has lived the majority of his life. Hady, an 18-year-old at the time of this publication — his first book —maintains dual citizenship in Egypt and the United States, and speaks fluent Arabic.

This book was designed and printed in the United States of America by House of Penguin on acid free paper comprised of recycled materials.
www.houseofpenguin.com